RENAL DIET COOKBOOK FOR BEGINNERS

RENAL DIET COOKBOOK FOR BEGINNERS – THE EXHAUSTIVE, COMPLETE AND EFFECTIVE MEAL PLAN FOR NEWLY DIAGNOSED MADE BY 250 LOW SODIUM, POTASSIUM, AND PHOSPHORUS RECIPES TO MAKE YOU EAT AND FEEL HEALTHIER

Sheila S. McManus

TABLE OF CONTENTS

INTRODUCTION

A renal diet is an eating plan exercised to help minimize waste products' levels in the blood. The renal diet is designed to cause as little work or stress on the kidneys as possible while still providing energy and the high nutrients the body needs.

A renal diet follows several fundamental guidelines. The first is that it must be a balanced, healthy, and sustainable diet, rich in natural grains, vitamins, fibers, carbohydrates, omega 3 fats, and fluids. Proteins should be adequate but not excessive.

Bad eating habits can have adverse effects on your health. If you want to avoid kidney diseases, you must manage a balanced diet and stay at a healthy weight. Your diet is supposed to contain low levels of fat and salt to control blood pressure. A diabetic person must control his/her blood sugar by choosing the right food and beverages. Control diabetes and high blood pressure to prevent the worse condition of kidney disease. Only a kidney-friendly diet can help you in the protection of kidneys from more damage. By choosing a kidney-friendly diet, you can limit particular foods to avoid the build-up of minerals in your body.

Salt or sodium is known for being one of the most important ingredients that the renal diet prohibits its use. This ingredient, although simple, can badly and strongly affect your body and especially the kidneys. Any excess of sodium can't be easily filtered because of the failing condition of the kidneys. A large build-up of sodium can cause catastrophic results on your body. Potassium and Phosphorus are also prohibited for kidney patients depending on the stage of kidney disease.

Kidney disease or in other words "renal disease" and "kidney damage" is a health condition where the kidneys are unable to function in a healthy and proper manner. Chronic kidney disease is a slow-moving disease and does not cause the patient a lot of complaints in the initial stages. Chronic kidney disease includes a group of kidney diseases, in which case the renal function decreases for several years or decades. With the help of timely diagnosis and treatment, it can slow down and even stop the progression of kidney disease.

Anatomically, the kidneys are positioned in the abdomen, at the back, usually on both sides of the spine. The renal artery, which is a direct branch of the aorta supplies blood to the kidneys. Renal veins empty the blood from kidneys to the vena cava, then the heart. The word "renal" originated from the Latin word for kidney.

There is a distinct connection between the health and function of our kidneys and the way we eat. How we eat and the foods we choose make a significant impact on how well we feel and our overall well-being. Making changes to your diet is often necessary to guard against medical conditions, and while eating well can treat existing conditions, healthy food choices can also help prevent many other conditions from developing – including kidney disease.

When we make changes to our diet, we often focus on the restrictions or foods we should avoid. While this is important, it's also vital to learn about the foods and nutrients we need in order to maintain good health and prevent disease. Consider the related conditions that contribute to high blood pressure and type 2 diabetes, and the dietary changes often suggested to treat and, in some successful cases, reverse the damage of these conditions. Dietary changes for the treatment and prevention of disease often focus on limiting salt, sugar, and trans fats from our food choices, while increasing minerals, protein, and fiber, among other beneficial nutrients. The renal diet also focuses on eliminating, or at least limiting, the consumption of various ingredients to aid our kidneys to function better and to prevent further damage from occurring.

CHAPTER 1. WHAT YOU NEED TO KNOW ABOUT KIDNEY DISEASE AND RENAL DIET

Before stepping further into the depths of the renal diet, let us learn more about our kidneys and how they function. This basic understanding can ensure a better awareness of kidney disease. Our kidneys act just like a filter; in fact, they are the natural filter of the body, which mainly filters the blood running into them with high pressure. There is one kidney on either side of the body; they both work in sync to clean and purify the entire body's blood constantly and consistently. The renal arteries that enter the kidneys also pass by the membranes in it, which only let the harmful excretory products to pass into the ureters of the kidneys and render the blood cleaned and purified. There is another vital function that the kidneys play which is to keep the water and electrolyte balance maintained in the body. If our body has water in excess, the kidneys will release it through urination, and if our body is dehydrated, then more water is retained. This smart mechanism is only possible when a critical mineral balance is maintained inside the kidney cells since the release of water can only occur through osmosis.

Kidney function or renal function are the terms used to explain how well the kidneys function. A healthy individual is born with a pair of kidneys. This is why whenever one of the kidneys lost its functioning it went unnoticed due to the function of the other kidney. But if the kidney functions further drop altogether and reach a level as low as 25 percent, it turns out to be serious for the patients. People who have only one kidney functioning need proper external therapy and in worst cases, a kidney transplant.

Kidney diseases occur when a number of renal cells known as nephrons are either partially or completely damaged and fail to filter blood entering in properly. The gradual damage of the kidney cells can occur due to various reasons, sometimes it is the acidic or toxic build-up inside the kidney over time, at times it is genetic, or the result of other kidney damaging diseases like hypertension (high blood pressure) or diabetes.

Chronic Kidney Disease (CKD)

CKD or chronic kidney disease is the stage of kidney damage where it fails to filter the blood properly. The term chronic is used to refer to gradual and long-term damage to an organ. Chronic kidney disease is therefore developed after a slow yet progressive damage to the kidneys. The symptoms of this disease only appear when the toxic wastes start to build up in the body. Therefore, such a stage should be prevented at all costs. Hence, early diagnosis of the disease proves to be significant. The sooner the patient realizes the gravity of the situation, the better measures he can take to curb the problem.

What are the causes of kidney disease?

There is never a single cause for a disease; a number of factors come into play and together become the source of the renal deficiency. As stated earlier, these causes may include the genetics of a person, some other health disorders that may damage the kidneys and the kind of lifestyle a person lives. The following are the most commonly known causes of renal disease.

• Heart disease

• Diabetes

• Hypertension (High blood pressure)

• Being around 60 years old

• Having kidney disease in family

Signs of renal disease

The good thing is that we can prevent the chronic stage of renal disease by identifying the early signs of any form of kidney damage. Even when a person feels minor changes in his body, he should consult an expert to confirm if it might lead to something serious. The following are a few of the early symptoms of renal damage:

• Tiredness or drowsiness

• Muscle cramps

• Loss of appetite

• Changes in the frequency of urination

• Swelling of hands and feet

• A feeling of itchiness

- Numbness

- The darkness of skin

- Trouble in sleeping

- Shortness of breath

- The feeling of nausea or vomiting

These symptoms can appear in combination with one another. These are general signs of body malfunction, and they should never be ignored. And if they are left unnoticed, they can lead to worsening of the condition and may appear as:

- Back pain

- Abdominal pain

- Fever

- Rash

- Diarrhea

- Nosebleeds

- Vomiting

After witnessing any of these symptoms, a person should immediately consult a health expert and prepare himself or herself for the required lifestyle changes.

Renal disease diagnostic tests

Besides identifying the symptoms of kidney disease, there are other better and more accurate ways to confirm the extent of loss of renal function. There are mainly two important diagnostic tests:

1. Urine test

The urine test clearly states all the renal problems. The urine is the waste product of the kidney. When there is loss of filtration or any hindrance to the kidneys, the urine sample will indicate it through the number of excretory products present in it. The severe stages of chronic disease show some amount of protein and blood in the urine. Do not rely on self-tests; visit an authentic clinic for these tests.

2. Blood pressure and blood test

Another good way to check for renal disease is to test the blood and its composition. A high amount of creatinine and other waste products in the blood clearly indicates that the kidneys are not functioning properly. Blood pressure can also be indicative of renal disease. When the water balance in the body is disturbed, it may cause high blood pressure. Hypertension can both be the cause and symptom of kidney disease and therefore should be taken seriously.

How to keep your kidneys healthy

Like all other parts of the body, human kidneys also need much care and attention to work effectively. It takes a few simple and consistent measures to keep them healthy. Remember that no medicine can guarantee good health, but only a better lifestyle can do so. Here are a few of the practices that can keep your kidneys stay healthy for life.

1. Active lifestyle

An active routine is imperative for good health. This may include regular exercise, yoga, or sports and physical activities. The more you move your body, the better its metabolism gets. The loss of water is compensated by drinking more water, and that constantly drains all the toxins and waste from the kidneys. It also helps in controlling blood pressure, cholesterol levels, and diabetes, which indirectly prevents kidney disease.

2. Control blood pressure

Constant high blood pressure may cause glomerular damage. It is one of the leading causes, and every 3 out of 5 people suffering from hypertension also suffer from kidney problems. The normal human blood pressure is below 120/80 mmHg. When there is a constant increase of this pressure up to 140/100mmHg or more it should be immediately put under control. This can be done by minimizing the salt intake, controlling the cholesterol level and taking care of cardiac health.

3. Hydration

Drinking more water and salt-free fluids proves to be the life support for kidneys. Water and fluids dilute the blood consistency and lead to more urination; this in turn will release most of the excretions out of the body without much difficulty. Drinking at least eight glasses of water in a day is essential. It is basically the lack of water which strains the kidneys and often hinders the glomerular filtration. Water is the best option, but fresh fruit juices with no salt and preservatives are also vital for kidney health. Keep all of them in constant daily use.

4. Dietary changes

There are certain food items which taken in excess can cause renal problems. In this regard, an extremely high protein diet, food rich in sodium, potassium, and phosphorous can be harmful. People who are suffering from early stages of renal disease should reduce their intake, whereas those facing critical stages of CKD should avoid their use altogether. A well-planned renal diet can prove to be significant in this regard. It effectively restricts all such food items from the diet and promotes the use of more fluids, water, organic fruits, and a low protein meal plan.

5. No smoking/alcohol

Smoking and excessive use of alcohol are other names for intoxication. Intoxication is another major cause of kidney disease, or at least it aggravates the condition. Smoking and drinking alcohol indirectly pollute the blood and body tissues, which leads to progressive kidney damage. Begin by gradually reducing alcohol consumption and smoking down to a minimum.

6. Monitor the changes

Since the early signs of kidney disease are hardly detectable, it is important to keep track of the changes you witness in your body. Even the frequency of urination and loss of appetite are good enough reasons to be cautious and concerning. It is true that only a health expert can accurately diagnose the disease, but personal care and attention to minor changes is of key importance when it comes to CKD.

CHAPTER 2. FOOD TO EAT AND TO AVOID

A renal diet focuses on foods that are natural and nutritious, but at the same time, are low in sodium, potassium, and phosphorus.

Foods to eat:

Cauliflower - 1 cup contains 19 mg sodium, 176 potassium, 40 mg phosphorus

Blueberries - 1 cup contains 1.5 mg sodium, 114 potassium, 18 mg phosphorus

Sea Bass - 3 ounces contain 74 mg sodium, 279 potassium, 211 mg phosphorus

Grapes - 1/2 cup contains 1.5 mg sodium, 144 potassium, 15 mg phosphorus

Egg Whites - 2 egg whites contain 110 mg sodium, 108 potassium, 10 mg phosphorus

Garlic - 3 cloves contain 1.5 mg sodium, 36 potassium, 14 mg phosphorus

Buckwheat - ½ cup contains 3.5 mg sodium, 74 potassium, 59 mg phosphorus

Olive Oil - 1 ounce 0.6 mg sodium, 0.3 potassium, 0 mg phosphorus

Bulgur - ½ cup contains 4.5 mg sodium, 62 potassium, 36 mg phosphorus

Cabbage - 1 cup contains 13 mg sodium, 119 potassium, 18 mg phosphorus

Skinless chicken - 3 ounces contain 63 mg sodium, 216 potassium, 192 mg phosphorus

Bell peppers - 1 piece contains 3 mg sodium, 156 potassium, 19 mg phosphorus

Onion - 1 piece contains 3 mg sodium, 102 potassium, 20 mg phosphorus

Arugula - 1 cup contains 6 mg sodium, 74 potassium, 10 mg phosphorus

Macadamia nuts - 1 ounce contains 1.4 mg sodium, 103 potassium, 53 mg phosphorus

Radish - ½ cup contains 23 mg sodium, 135 potassium, 12 mg phosphorus

Turnips - ½ cup contains 12.5 mg sodium, 138 potassium, 20 mg phosphorus

Pineapple - 1 cup contains 2 mg sodium, 180 potassium, 13 mg phosphorus

Cranberries – 1 cup contains 2 mg sodium, 85 potassium, 13 mg phosphorus

Mushrooms – 1 cup contains 6 mg sodium, 170 potassium, 42 mg phosphorus

Foods to Avoid

These foods are known to have high levels of potassium, sodium, or phosphorus:

Soda – Soda is believed to contain up to 100 mg of additive phosphorus per 200 ml.

Avocados - 1 cup contains up to 727 mg of potassium.

Canned foods – Canned foods contain high amounts of sodium, so make sure that you avoid using these, or at least opt for low-sodium versions.

Whole wheat bread – 1 ounce of bread contains 57 mg phosphorus and 69 mg potassium, which is higher compared to white bread.

Brown rice – 1 cup of brown rice contains 154 mg potassium, while 1 cup of white rice only has 54 mg potassium.

Bananas – 1 banana contains 422 mg of potassium.

Dairy – Dairy products are high in potassium, phosphorus, and calcium. You can still consume dairy products, but you have to limit it. Use dairy milk alternatives like almond milk and coconut milk.

Processed Meats – Processed meats are not advisable for people with kidney problems because of their high content of additives and preservatives.

Pickled and cured foods – These are made using large amounts of salt.

Apricots – 1 cup contains 427 mg potassium.

Potatoes and sweet potatoes – 1 potato contain 610 mg potassium. You can double boil potatoes and sweet potatoes to reduce potassium by 50 percent.

Tomatoes – 1 cup tomato sauce contains up to 900 mg potassium.

Instant meals – Instant meals are known for extremely high amounts of sodium.

Spinach – Spinach contains up to 290 mg potassium per cup. Cooking helps reduce the amount of potassium.

Raisins, prunes, and dates – Dried fruits have concentrated nutrients, including potassium. 1 cup of prunes contain up to 1,274 mg potassium.

Chips – Chips are known to have high amounts of sodium.

Since the Renal Diet is generally a Low Sodium, Low Phosphorus program, there are certain health benefits that you will enjoy from this diet. (Apart from improving your kidney health). Some of the crucial ones are as follows:

- It helps to lower blood pressure

- It helps to lower your LDL cholesterol

- It helps to lower your risk of having a heart attack

- It helps to prevent heart failure

- It decreases the possibility of having a stroke

- It helps to protect your vision

- It helps to improve your memory

- It helps to lower the possibility of dementia

It helps to build stronger bones

CHAPTER 3. BREAKFAST RECIPES

1. APPLE CHERRY BREAKFAST RISOTTO

PREPARATION: 10 MIN **COOKING: 15 MIN** **SERVES: 1**

INGREDIENTS

- 2 large apples, cored and chopped
- 1 ½ cups arborio rice
- ½ cup dried cherries
- 1 ½ tsp cinnamon
- 2 tbsp butter
- ¼ tsp salt
- 1 cup apple juice
- 3 cups of milk

DIRECTIONS

1. Add butter to the pressure-cooking pot and heat for 2 to 3 minutes.
2. Whisk in the rice, continue heating, and consistently whisk until rice darkens for about 3 to 4 minutes.
3. Put the spices, brown sugar, and apples.
4. Whisk in the juice and milk.
5. Set pressure cooker to high pressure and select 6 minutes cook time and heat.
6. Once the timer beeps, unplug the cooker and use a fast pressure release to release the pressure.
7. Gently remove the lid of the pressure cooker and whisk in dried cherries.
8. Serve hot, and garnish with extra sliced almonds, brown sugar, and milk.

Nutritions: *Calories: 258 Fat: 3g Carbs: 50g Protein: 10g Sodium: 227mg Potassium: 580mg Phosphorus: 150mg*

2. BERRIES AND CREAM BREAKFAST CAKE

PREPARATION: 15 MIN

COOKING: 35 MIN

SERVES: 1

INGREDIENTS

- 5 eggs
- ¼ cup of sugar
- 2 tbsp butter, melted
- ¾ cup ricotta cheese
- Sweet yogurt glaze
- Berry Compote
- 2 tsp vanilla extract
- ½ tsp salt
- 1 cup of whole white wheat flour or wheat pastry flour
- 2 tsp baking powder
- ½ cup berry compote

For the sweet yogurt glaze
- ½ tsp vanilla extract
- ¼ cup yogurt
- 1 to 2 tbsp powdered sugar
- 1 tsp milk

DIRECTIONS

1. First, make ready the berry compote to chill and become thick.
2. For the cake, thoroughly oil a pan with a non-stick cooking spray.
3. Mix the eggs and sugar until blended.
4. Add the ricotta cheese, butter, vanilla, yogurt, and stir until blended.
5. Mix salt, baking powder, and the flour in a separate bowl.
6. Add to the egg mixture. Turn into the prepared pan.
7. With a tablespoon, drop 1/2 cup of berry compote on top of the batter and whisk with a knife.
8. Turn 1 cup of water in the pressure cooker pot and set in the steamer basket. Gently position the pan on the steamer basket.
9. Set the pressure to high. Heat for about 25 minutes.
10. While cooking the cake, prepare the sweet yogurt glaze by mixing the vanilla, yogurt, powdered sugar, and milk.
11. Keep aside. Once cooking is completed, use a normal release to vent pressure for 10 minutes and then release any further pressure.
12. Take out the pan from the pressure cooker. Allow chilling a bit. Loosen the edges of the cake off the pan and lightly pour on a plate.
13. Sprinkle with sweet yogurt glaze and serve hot.

Nutritions: *Calories: 275 Fat: 13g Carbs: 36g Protein: 5g Sodium: 110.8mg Potassium: 175.6mg Phosphorus: 78mg*

3. TURKEY AND SPINACH SCRAMBLE ON MELBA TOAST

PREPARATION: 5 MIN

COOKING: 15 MIN

SERVES: 2

INGREDIENTS

- 1 tsp. Extra virgin olive oil
- 1 cup Raw spinach
- ½ clove, minced Garlic
- 1 tsp. grated Nutmeg
- 1 cup Cooked and diced turkey breast
- 4 slices Melba toast
- 1 tsp. Balsamic vinegar

DIRECTIONS

1. Heat a skillet over medium heat and add oil.
2. Add turkey and heat through for 6 to 8 minutes.
3. Add spinach, garlic, and nutmeg and stir-fry for 6 minutes more.
4. Plate up the Melba toast and top with spinach and turkey scramble.
5. Drizzle with balsamic vinegar and serve.

Nutritions: *Calories: 301 Fat: 19g Carb: 12g Protein: 19g Sodium: 360mg Potassium: 269mg Phosphorus: 215mg*

4. CHEESY SCRAMBLED EGGS WITH FRESH HERBS

PREPARATION: 15 MIN

COOKING: 10 MIN

SERVES: 4

INGREDIENTS

- 3 Eggs
- 2 Egg whites
- ½ cup Cream cheese
- ¼ cup Unsweetened rice milk
- 1 tbsp. green part only Chopped scallion
- 1 tbsp. Chopped fresh tarragon
- 2 tbsps. Unsalted butter
- Ground black pepper to taste

DIRECTIONS

1. Whisk the eggs, egg whites, cream cheese, rice milk, scallions, and tarragon. Mix until smooth.
2. Melt the butter in a skillet.
3. Put egg mixture and cook for 5 minutes or until the eggs are thick and curds creamy.
4. Season with pepper and serve.

Nutritions: *Calories: 221 Fat: 19g Carb: 3g Protein: 8g Sodium: 193mg Potassium: 140mg Phosphorus: 119mg*

5. MEXICAN STYLE BURRITOS

PREPARATION: 5 MIN   **COOKING: 15 MIN**   **SERVES: 2**

INGREDIENTS

- 1 tbsp. Olive oil
- 2 Corn tortillas
- ¼ cup chopped Red onion
- ¼ cup chopped Red bell peppers
- ½, deseeded and chopped red chili
- 2 Eggs
- 1 lime juice
- 1 tbsp. chopped Cilantro

DIRECTIONS

1. Place the tortillas in medium heat for 1 to 2 minutes on each side or until lightly toasted.
2. Remove and keep the broiler on.
3. Heat the oil in a skillet and sauté onion, chili, and bell peppers for 5 to 6 minutes or until soft.
4. Crack the eggs over the top of the onions and peppers.
5. Place skillet under the broiler for 5 to 6 minutes or until the eggs are cooked.
6. Serve half the eggs and vegetables on top of each tortilla and sprinkle with cilantro and lime juice to serve.

Nutritions: *Calories: 202 Fat: 13g Carb: 19g Protein: 9g Sodium: 77mg Potassium: 233mg Phosphorus: 184mg*

6. BULGUR, COUSCOUS, AND BUCKWHEAT CEREAL

PREPARATION: 10 MIN

COOKING: 25 MIN

SERVES: 4

INGREDIENTS

- 2 ¼ cups Water
- 1 ¼ cups Vanilla rice milk
- 6 Tbsps. Uncooked bulgur
- 2 Tbsps. Uncooked whole buckwheat
- 1 cup Sliced apple
- 6 Tbsps. Plain uncooked couscous
- ½ tsp. Ground cinnamon

DIRECTIONS

1. Heat the water and milk in the saucepan over medium heat. Let it boil.
2. Put the bulgur, buckwheat, and apple.
3. Reduce the heat to low and simmer, occasionally stirring until the bulgur is tender, about 20 to 25 minutes.
4. Remove the saucepan and stir in the couscous and cinnamon—cover for 10 minutes.
5. Put the cereal before serving.

Nutritions: *Calories: 159 Fat: 1g Carb: 34g Protein: 4g Sodium: 33mg Potassium: 116m Phosphorus: 130mg*

7. BLUEBERRY MUFFINS

PREPARATION: 15 MIN

COOKING: 30 MIN

SERVES: 12

INGREDIENTS

- 2 cups Unsweetened rice milk
- 1 Tbsp. Apple cider vinegar
- 3 ½ cups All-purpose flour
- 1 cup Granulated sugar
- 1 Tbsp. Baking soda substitute
- 1 tsp. Ground cinnamon
- ½ tsp. Ground nutmeg
- Pinch ground ginger
- ½ cup Canola oil
- 2 Tbsps. Pure vanilla extract
- 2 ½ cups Fresh blueberries

DIRECTIONS

1. Preheat the oven to 375F.
2. Prepare a muffin pan and set aside.
3. Stir together the rice milk and vinegar in a small bowl. Set aside for 10 minutes.
4. In a large bowl, stir together the sugar, flour, baking soda, cinnamon, nutmeg, and ginger until well mixed.
5. Add oil and vanilla to the milk and mix.
6. Put milk mixture to dry ingredients and stir well to combine.
7. Put the blueberries and spoon the muffin batter evenly into the cups.
8. Bake the muffins for 25 to 30 minutes or until golden and a toothpick inserted comes out clean.
9. Cool for 15 minutes and serve.

Nutritions: *Calories: 331 Fat: 11g Carb: 52g Protein: 6g Sodium: 35mg Potassium: 89mg Phosphorus: 90mg*

8. BUCKWHEAT AND GRAPEFRUIT PORRIDGE

PREPARATION: 5 MIN **COOKING: 20 MIN** **SERVES: 2**

INGREDIENTS

- ½ cup Buckwheat
- ¼ chopped Grapefruit
- 1 Tbsp. Honey
- 1 ½ cups Almond milk
- 2 cups Water

DIRECTIONS

1. Let the water boil on the stove. Add the buckwheat and place the lid on the pan.
2. Lower heat slightly and simmer for 7 to 10 minutes, checking to ensure water does not dry out.
3. When most of the water is absorbed, remove, and set aside for 5 minutes.
4. Drain any excess water from the pan and stir in almond milk, heating through for 5 minutes.
5. Add the honey and grapefruit.
6. Serve.

Nutritions: *Calories: 231 Fat: 4g Carb: 43g Protein: 13g Sodium: 135mg Potassium: 370mg Phosphorus: 165mg*

9. EGG AND VEGGIE MUFFINS

PREPARATION: 15 MIN

COOKING: 20 MIN

SERVES: 4

INGREDIENTS

- 4 Eggs
- 2 Tbsp. Unsweetened rice milk
- ½ chopped Sweet onion
- ½ chopped Red bell pepper
- Pinch red pepper flakes
- Pinch ground black pepper

DIRECTIONS

1. Preheat the oven to 350F.
2. Spray 4 muffin pans with cooking spray. Set aside.
3. Whisk the milk, eggs, onion, red pepper, parsley, red pepper flakes, and black pepper until mixed.
4. Pour the egg mixture into prepared muffin pans.
5. Bake until the muffins are puffed and golden, about 18 to 20 minutes. Serve.

Nutritions: *Calories: 84 Fat: 5g Carb: 3g Protein: 7g Sodium: 75mg Potassium: 117mg Phosphorus: 110mg*

10. BERRY CHIA WITH YOGURT

PREPARATION: 35 MIN

COOKING: 5 MIN

SERVES: 4

INGREDIENTS

- ½ cup chia seeds, dried
- 2 cup Plain yogurt
- 1/3 cup strawberries, chopped
- ¼ cup blackberries
- ¼ cup raspberries
- 4 teaspoons Splenda

DIRECTIONS

1. Mix up together Plain yogurt with Splenda, and chia seeds.
2. Transfer the mixture into the serving ramekins (jars) and leave for 35 minutes.
3. After this, add blackberries, raspberries, and strawberries. Mix up the meal well.
4. Serve it immediately or store it in the fridge for up to 2 days.

Nutritions: *Calories: 150 Fat: 5g Carbs: 19g Protein: 6.8g Sodium: 65mg Potassium: 226mg Phosphorus: 75mg*

11. ARUGULA EGGS WITH CHILI PEPPERS

PREPARATION: 7 MIN

COOKING: 10 MIN

SERVES: 4

INGREDIENTS

- 2 cups arugula, chopped
- 3 eggs, beaten
- ½ chili pepper, chopped
- 1 tablespoon butter
- 1 oz Parmesan, grated

DIRECTIONS

1. Toss butter in the skillet and melt it.
2. Add arugula and sauté it over medium heat for 5 minutes. Stir it from time to time.
3. Meanwhile, mix up together Parmesan, chili pepper, and eggs.
4. Pour the egg mixture over the arugula and scramble well.
5. Cook for 5 minutes more over medium heat.

Nutritions: *Calories: 218 Fat: 15g Carbs: 2.8g Protein: 17g Sodium: 656mg Potassium: 243mg Phosphorus: 310mg*

12. EGGPLANT CHICKEN SANDWICH

PREPARATION: 10 MIN **COOKING: 15 MIN** **SERVES: 2**

INGREDIENTS

- 1 eggplant, trimmed
- 10 oz chicken fillet
- 1 teaspoon Plain yogurt
- ½ teaspoon minced garlic
- 1 tablespoon fresh cilantro, chopped
- 2 lettuce leaves
- 1 teaspoon olive oil
- ½ teaspoon salt
- ½ teaspoon chili pepper
- 1 teaspoon butter

DIRECTIONS

1. Slice the eggplant lengthwise into 4 slices.
2. Rub the eggplant slices with minced garlic and brush with olive oil.
3. Grill the eggplant slices on the preheated to 375F grill for 3 minutes from each side.
4. Meanwhile, rub the chicken fillet with salt and chili pepper.
5. Place it in the skillet and add butter.
6. Roast the chicken for 6 minutes from each side over medium-high heat.
7. Cool the cooked eggplants gently and spread one side of them with Plain yogurt.
8. Add lettuce leaves and chopped fresh cilantro.
9. After this, slice the cooked chicken fillet and add over the lettuce.
10. Cover it with the remaining sliced eggplant to get the sandwich shape. Pin the sandwich with the toothpick if needed.

Nutritions: *Calories: 276 Fat: 11g Carbs: 41g Protein: 13.8g Sodium: 775mg Potassium: 532mg Phosphorus: 187mg*

13. EGGS IN TOMATO RINGS

PREPARATION: 8 MIN

COOKING: 5 MIN

SERVES: 2

INGREDIENTS

- 1 tomato
- 2 eggs
- ¼ teaspoon chili flakes
- ¾ teaspoon salt
- ½ teaspoon butter

DIRECTIONS

1. Trim the tomato and slice it into 2 rings.
2. Remove the tomato flesh.
3. Toss butter in the skillet and melt it.
4. Then arrange the tomato rings.
5. Crack the eggs in the tomato rings. Sprinkle them with salt and chili flakes.
6. Cook the eggs for 4 minutes over medium heat with the closed lid.
7. Transfer the cooked eggs into the serving plates with the help of the spatula.

Nutritions: *Calories: 237 Fat: 16g Carbs: 7g Protein: 16g Sodium: 427mg Potassium: 391.5mg Phosphorus: 291mg*

14. CHORIZO BOWL WITH CORN

PREPARATION: 10 MIN

COOKING: 15 MIN

SERVES: 4

INGREDIENTS

- 9 oz chorizo
- 1 tablespoon almond butter
- ½ cup corn kernels
- 1 tomato, chopped
- ¾ cup heavy cream
- 1 teaspoon butter
- ¼ teaspoon chili pepper
- 1 tablespoon dill, chopped

DIRECTIONS

1. Chop the chorizo and place it in the skillet.
2. Add almond butter and chili pepper.
3. Roast the chorizo for 3 minutes.
4. After this, add tomato and corn kernels.
5. Add butter and chopped the dill. Mix up the mixture well—Cook for 2 minutes.
6. Close the lid and simmer for 10 minutes over low heat.
7. Transfer the cooked meal into the serving bowls.

Nutritions: *Calories: 286 Fat: 15g Carbs: 26g Protein: 13g Sodium: 228mg Potassium: 255mg Phosphorus: 293mg*

15. PANZANELLA SALAD

PREPARATION: 10 MIN **COOKING: 5 MIN** **SERVES: 4**

INGREDIENTS

- 3 tomatoes, chopped
- 2 cucumbers, chopped
- 1 red onion, sliced
- 2 red bell peppers, chopped
- ¼ cup fresh cilantro, chopped
- 1 tablespoon capers
- 1 oz whole-grain bread, chopped
- 1 tablespoon canola oil
- ½ teaspoon minced garlic
- 1 tablespoon Dijon mustard
- 1 teaspoon olive oil
- 1 teaspoon lime juice

DIRECTIONS

1. Pour canola oil into the skillet and bring it to boil.
2. Add chopped bread and roast it until crunchy (3-5 minutes).
3. Meanwhile, in the salad bowl, combine sliced red onion, cucumbers, tomatoes, bell peppers, cilantro, capers, and mix up gently.
4. Make the dressing: mix up together lime juice, olive oil, Dijon mustard, and minced garlic.
5. Put the dressing over the salad and stir it directly before serving.

Nutritions: *Calories: 224.3 Fat: 10g Carbs: 26g Protein: 6.6g Sodium: 401mg Potassium: 324.9mg Phosphorus: 84mg*

16. POACHED ASPARAGUS AND EGG

PREPARATION: 3 MIN   **COOKING: 15 MIN**   **SERVES: 1**

INGREDIENTS

- 1 egg
- 4 spears asparagus
- Water

DIRECTIONS

1. Half-fill a deep saucepan with water set over high heat. Let the water come to a boil.
2. Dip asparagus spears in water. Cook until they turn a shade brighter, about 3 minutes. Remove from saucepan and drain on paper towels. Keep warm—lightly season before serving.
3. Use a slotted spoon to lower the egg into boiling water gently.
4. Cook for only 4 minutes. Remove from pan immediately. Place on egg holder.
5. Slice off the top. The egg should still be fluid inside.
6. Place asparagus spears on a small plate and serve egg on the side.
7. Dip asparagus into the egg and eat while warm.

Nutritions: *Calories: 178 Fat: 13g Carbs: 1g Protein: 7.72g Calories 178 Sodium: 71mg Potassium: 203mg Phosphorus: 124mg*

17. EGG DROP SOUP

PREPARATION: 5 MIN

COOKING: 10 MIN

SERVES: 4

INGREDIENTS

- ¼ cup minced fresh chives
- 4 cups unsalted vegetable stock
- 4 whisked eggs

DIRECTIONS

1. Pour unsalted vegetable stock into the oven set over high heat. Bring to a boil. Lower heat.
2. Pour in the eggs. Stir until ribbons form into the soup.
3. Turn off the heat immediately. The residual heat will cook eggs through.
4. Cool slightly before ladling the desired amount into individual bowls. Garnish with a pinch of parsley, if using.
5. Serve immediately.

Nutritions: *Calories: 73 Fat: 3g Carbs: 1g Protein: 7g Sodium: 891mg Potassium: 53mg Phosphorus: 36mg*

18. TASTY BEEF AND LIVER BURGER

PREPARATION: 5 MIN

COOKING: 5 MIN

SERVES: 4

INGREDIENTS

- ½ medium red onion, peeled
- 1 tsp sea salt
- 1 tsp poultry seasoning
- ¼ pound chicken livers
- pounds beef
- 1 ½ tsp coriander
- 1 tsp ground black pepper

DIRECTIONS

1. Add the onion and chicken liver to a food processor and process until blended.
2. Put in the ground beef and all the ingredients.
3. Blend for about 1 minute until the ingredients combined thoroughly.
4. Mold the mixture into four-inch wide patties.
5. Broil patties until it is done to your desired taste.
6. Serve on a lettuce wrap or hamburger and enjoy it.

Nutritions: *Calories: 220 Fat: 4g Protein: 23g Sodium: 78mg Potassium: 344.7mg Phosphorus: 461mg*

19. CREAMY KETO CUCUMBER SALAD

PREPARATION: 5 MIN

COOKING: 5 MIN

SERVES: 1

INGREDIENTS

- 2 tbsp of mayo
- Freshly ground pepper
- 2 tbsp lemon juice
- 1 cucumber about 220grams, sliced

DIRECTIONS

1. Combine the mayo, lemon juice, and cucumber strips in a medium bowl
2. Put salt and pepper to taste.
3. Serve and enjoy.

Nutritions: *Calories: 77 Fat: 5g Carbs: 6g Protein: 1g Sodium: 150mg Potassium: 99mg Phosphorus: 17mg*

20. SHREDDED CHICKEN CHILI

PREPARATION: 10 MIN

COOKING: 25 MIN

SERVES: 1

INGREDIENTS

- 1 tbsp butter
- 1 jalapeno pepper, diced
- 2 oz tomato paste
- ½ tbsp garlic powder
- 10 oz diced tomatoes canned
- Salt and pepper to taste
- 4 chicken breasts, shredded
- 1 tbsp chili powder
- 2 cups chicken broth
- 4 oz cream cheese
- ½ onion, diced
- 1 tbsp cumin

DIRECTIONS

1. Add chicken breast and water to a sizable pot and bring to a boil for 10 to 12 minutes.
2. Once well cooked, take out of the heat and crumble with two forks.
3. Add butter to a large pot and melt over medium to high heat.
4. Add onion and sauté until tender.
5. Add the chicken broth, chili powder, shredded chicken, garlic powder, cumin, and jalapeno to the pot and stir well until evenly blended.
6. Cook over medium to low heat and cover with lid for 10 minutes.
7. Chop cream cheese into 1-inch small strips.
8. Remove the cover and whisk in the cream cheese. Increase the heat to medium-high and keep on whisking until the cream cheese combined thoroughly.
9. Take out of the heat and add salt and pepper to taste. Serve and sprinkle with any desired toppings and enjoy.

Nutritions: *Calories: 330 Fat: 2.8g Carbs: 38g Protein: 38g Sodium: 716mg Potassium: 970.7mg Phosphorus: 421mg*

21. SPINACH, GOAT CHEESE & CHORIZO OMELET

PREPARATION: 5 MIN

COOKING: 10 MIN

SERVES: 1

INGREDIENTS

- 4 eggs
- 4 ounces chorizo sausage
- ½ tbsp butter
- 1/4 cup salsa Verde (optional)
- 1 tbsp water
- 2 cups baby spinach leaves
- 2 ounces shredded fresh goat cheese
- Avocado, diced

DIRECTIONS

1. In a medium-sized frying pan, take out chorizo from the casing and sauté until thoroughly cooked.
2. Meanwhile, add water to a small bowl and beat in the eggs.
3. Remove the chorizo from the skillet with a spoon and keep aside. Clean off the skillet of the remaining oil with a paper towel.
4. Over a moderate flame, melt the butter in the same skillet.
5. Put the cracked eggs in the skillet, and then add the spinach, chorizo, and shredded goat cheese to half of the mixture of the eggs.
6. Heat on low flame for about 3 minutes until a bit dense, then add in the filling and fold over.
7. Cover the skillet with a pot cover and cook on a moderate flame for few minutes until the eggs are evenly cooked.
8. Turn off the stove and allow skillet cover for about 8 minutes while it gets cooked with the extra heat. Serve with slices of avocado and salsa.

Nutritions: *Calories: 324 Fat: 15.5g Carbs: 26g Protein: 21g Sodium: 389mg Potassium: 501.3mg Phosphorus: 238mg*

22. EGG AND BROCCOLI CASSEROLE

PREPARATION: 15 MIN **COOKING: 3 H** **SERVES: 1**

INGREDIENTS

- ½ tsp salt
- 3 cups frozen, sliced broccoli, thawed and drained
- 6 eggs
- 3 tbsp thinly sliced onion
- 2 cups crumbled cheddar cheese
- ¼ cup butter softened
- 3 cups of cottage cheese
- Extra crumbled cheddar cheese, optional
- 1/3 cup all-purpose flour

DIRECTIONS

1. Combine all the ingredients in a sizable bowl. Turn into a greased instant pot.
2. Set in the lid and cook on high for 1 hour, then whisk.
3. Lower the heat, place in the lid and cook for an additional 2 hours 30 minutes to 3 hours until a thermometer shows 160 degrees.
4. Unplug the cooker, take out your meal and spread in cheese, and enjoy.

Nutritions: *Calories: 260 Fat: 13g Carbs: 10g Protein: 23g Sodium: 335mg Potassium: 161.6mg Phosphorus: 82.8mg*

23. SPINACH AND HAM FRITTATA

PREPARATION: 15 MIN

COOKING: 2-3 H

SERVES: 1

INGREDIENTS

- 1 tsp coconut oil
- 8 eggs, whisked
- ½ tsp pepper
- 1 small onion, sliced
- 1 tsp sea salt
- 2 cloves garlic
- 2 cups spinach, diced
- 1 cup ham, sliced
- ½ cup of canned coconut milk

DIRECTIONS

1. Melt coconut oil in a medium pan.
2. Put onion and garlic and cook until softened.
3. Pour the mixture of the garlic and onion in the instant pot.
4. Add in the ham and spinach.
5. Whisk ingredients until well blended.
6. In a separate bowl, combine coconut milk, whisked egg mixture, salt, pepper, and whisked with a stirrer until well blended.
7. Turn the mixture into the cooking pot and stir well.
8. Set the cooker to low and cook for 4 to 6 hours until the egg is set. You can as well set to high and cook for 2 to 3 hours.
9. Once done, serve warm and enjoy.

Nutritions: *Calories: 390 Fat: 24g Carbs: 6g Protein: 35g Sodium: 847mg Potassium: 145.9mg Phosphorus: 41mg*

24. HOT FRUIT SALAD

PREPARATION: 10 MIN   **COOKING: 2-3 H**   **SERVES: 1**

INGREDIENTS

- ¾ cups of sugar
- ¼ tsp ground nutmeg
- ¼ cup dried cranberries
- ½ cup butter, melted
- ¼ tsp ground cinnamon
- 1/8 tsp salt
- ½ cup dried apricots, sliced
- 2 (15 1/4-ounce) cans of chopped peaches, drained
- 2 (15 1/4-ounce) cans of diced pears, not drained
- One 23-ounce jar of chunky applesauce

DIRECTIONS

1. Mix the butter, sugar, nutmeg, cinnamon, and salt in the instant pot.
2. Turn in the rest ingredients.
3. Place in the lid and cook on high until evenly cooked.
4. Allow cooling and then serve.

Nutritions: *Calories: 152 Fat: 0.1g Carbs: 39g Protein: 0.7g Sodium: 15mg Potassium: 220.6mg Phosphorus: 21mg*

25. BACON AND CHEESE QUICHE

PREPARATION: 5 MIN

COOKING: 4 H

SERVES: 1

INGREDIENTS

- 1 cup milk
- ¼ tsp salt
- ¼ tsp freshly ground pepper
- 1 box refrigerated pie crusts
- 6 eggs
- 1 cup cooked bacon
- 2 cups crumbled Monterrey jack cheese

DIRECTIONS

1. Grease 5 to 6-quart slow oval cooker with a cooking spray.
2. Press halves of pie crust 2 inches up the side and halve in the bottom in the cooker, to extend over seams by 1/4 inch.
3. Heat for 1 hour 30 minutes on high.
4. Turn in stirred eggs and bacon over the mixture.
5. Garnish with cheese and seasonings.
6. Heat on low for 2 hours 30 minutes

Nutritions: *Calories: 524 Fat: 34g Carbs: 22g Protein: 25g Sodium: 826mg Potassium: 174.8mg Phosphorus: 287.1mg*

CHAPTER 4. LUNCH RECIPES

26. GREEK SALAD

PREPARATION: 10 MIN **COOKING: 0 MIN** **SERVES: 2**

INGREDIENTS

- 2 cups lettuce leaves
- 4 oz black olives
- 2 tomatoes
- 2 cucumbers
- 1 tablespoon lemon juice
- 1 teaspoon olive oil
- ¼ teaspoon dried oregano
- ½ teaspoon salt
- ¼ teaspoon chili flakes
- 4 oz Feta cheese

DIRECTIONS

1. Chop Feta cheese into the small cubes.
2. Chop the lettuce leaves roughly put them in the salad bowl.
3. Slice black olives and add them in the lettuce.
4. Then chop tomatoes and cucumbers into the cubes. Add them in the lettuce bowl.
5. For the dressing: whisk together chili flakes, salt, dried oregano, olive oil, and lemon juice.
6. Pour the dressing over the lettuce mixture and mix up well.
7. Sprinkle the salad with Feta cubes and shake gently.

Nutritions: *Calories 312, Fat 21.2, Fiber 5.3, Carbs 23.5, Protein 11.9*
Phosphorus: 120mg Potassium: 117mg Sodium: 65mg

27. SAUTÉED CHICKPEA AND LENTIL MIX

PREPARATION: 10 MIN **COOKING: 50 MIN** **SERVES: 4**

INGREDIENTS

- 1 cup chickpeas, half-cooked
- 1 cup lentils
- 5 cups chicken stock
- ½ cup fresh cilantro, chopped
- 1 teaspoon salt
- ½ teaspoon chili flakes
- ¼ cup onion, diced
- 1 tablespoon tomato paste

DIRECTIONS

1. Place chickpeas in the pan.
2. Add water, salt, and chili flakes.
3. Boil the chickpeas for 30 minutes over the medium heat.
4. Then add diced onion, lentils, and tomato paste. Stir well.
5. Close the lid and cook the mix for 15 minutes.
6. After this, add chopped cilantro, stir the meal well and cook it for 5 minutes more.
7. Let the cooked lunch chill little before serving.

Nutritions: *Calories 370, Fat 4.3, Fiber 23.7, Carbs 61.6, Protein 23.2 Phosphorus: 110mg Potassium: 117mg Sodium: 75mg*

28. CRAZY JAPANESE POTATO AND BEEF CROQUETTES

PREPARATION: 10 MIN

COOKING: 20 MIN

SERVES: 10

INGREDIENTS

- 3 medium russet potatoes, peeled and chopped
- 1 tablespoon almond butter
- 1 tablespoon vegetable oil
- 3 onions, diced
- ¾ pound ground beef
- 4 teaspoons light coconut aminos
- All-purpose flour for coating
- 2 eggs, beaten
- Panko bread crumbs for coating
- ½ cup oil, frying

DIRECTIONS

1. Take a saucepan and place it over medium-high heat; add potatoes and sunflower seeds water, boil for 16 minutes.
2. Remove water and put potatoes in another bowl, add almond butter and mash the potatoes.
3. Take a frying pan and place it over medium heat, add 1 tablespoon oil and let it heat up.
4. Add onions and stir fry until tender.
5. Add coconut aminos to beef to onions.
6. Keep frying until beef is browned.
7. Mix the beef with the potatoes evenly.
8. Take another frying pan and place it over medium heat; add half a cup of oil.
9. Form croquettes using the mashed potato mixture and coat them with flour, then eggs and finally breadcrumbs.
10. Fry patties until golden on all sides.
11. Enjoy!

Nutritions: *Calories: 239 Fat: 4g Carbohydrates: 20g Protein: 10g Phosphorus: 120mg Potassium: 107mg Sodium: 75mg*

29. SPICY CHILI CRACKERS

PREPARATION: 15 MIN   **COOKING: 60 MIN**   **SERVES: 30 CRACKERS**

INGREDIENTS

- ¾ cup almond flour
- ¼ cup coconut four
- ¼ cup coconut flour
- ½ teaspoon paprika
- ½ teaspoon cumin
- 1 ½ teaspoons chili pepper spice
- 1 teaspoon onion powder
- ½ teaspoon sunflower seeds
- 1 whole egg
- ¼ cup unsalted almond butter

DIRECTIONS

1. Preheat your oven to 350 degrees F.
2. Line a baking sheet with parchment paper and keep it on the side.
3. Add ingredients to your food processor and pulse until you have a nice dough.
4. Divide dough into two equal parts.
5. Place one ball on a sheet of parchment paper and cover with another sheet; roll it out.
6. Cut into crackers and repeat with the other ball.
7. Transfer the prepped dough to a baking tray and bake for 8-10 minutes.
8. Remove from oven and serve.
9. Enjoy!

Nutritions: *Total Carbs: 2.8g Fiber: 1g Protein: 1.6g Fat: 4.1g Phosphorus: 130mg Potassium: 127mg Sodium: 75mg*

30. TRADITIONAL BLACK BEAN CHILI

PREPARATION: 10 MIN **COOKING: 4 H** **SERVES: 4**

INGREDIENTS

- 1 ½ cups red bell pepper, chopped
- 1 cup yellow onion, chopped
- 1 ½ cups mushrooms, sliced
- 1 tablespoon olive oil
- 1 tablespoon chili powder
- 2 garlic cloves, minced
- 1 teaspoon chipotle chili pepper, chopped
- ½ teaspoon cumin, ground
- 16 ounces canned black beans, drained and rinsed
- 2 tablespoons cilantro, chopped
- 1 cup tomatoes, chopped

DIRECTIONS

1. Add red bell peppers, onion, dill, mushrooms, chili powder, garlic, chili pepper, cumin, black beans, tomatoes to your Slow Cooker.
2. Stir well.
3. Place lid and cook on HIGH for 4 hours.
4. Sprinkle cilantro on top.
5. Serve and enjoy!

Nutritions: *Calories: 211 Fat: 3g Carbohydrates: 22g Protein: 5g Phosphorus: 90mg Potassium: 107mg Sodium: 75mg*

31. VERY WILD MUSHROOM PILAF

PREPARATION: 10 MIN

COOKING: 3 H

SERVES: 4

INGREDIENTS

- 1 cup wild rice
- 2 garlic cloves, minced
- 6 green onions, chopped
- 2 tablespoons olive oil
- ½ pound baby Bella mushrooms
- 2 cups water

DIRECTIONS

1. Add rice, garlic, onion, oil, mushrooms and water to your Slow Cooker.
2. Stir well until mixed.
3. Place lid and cook on LOW for 3 hours.
4. Stir pilaf and divide between serving platters.
5. Enjoy!

Nutritions: *Calories: 210 Fat: 7g Carbohydrates: 16g Protein: 4g Phosphorus: 130mg Potassium: 127mg Sodium: 75mg*

32. GREEN PALAK PANEER

PREPARATION: 5 MIN **COOKING: 10 MIN** **SERVES: 4**

INGREDIENTS

- 1-pound spinach
- 2 cups cubed paneer (vegan)
- 2 tablespoons coconut oil
- 1 teaspoon cumin
- 1 chopped up onion
- 1-2 teaspoons hot green chili minced up
- 1 teaspoon minced garlic
- 15 cashews
- 4 tablespoons almond milk
- 1 teaspoon Garam masala
- Flavored vinegar as needed

DIRECTIONS

1. Add cashews and milk to a blender and blend well.
2. Set your pot to Sauté mode and add coconut oil; allow the oil to heat up.
3. Add cumin seeds, garlic, green chilies, ginger and sauté for 1 minute.
4. Add onion and sauté for 2 minutes.
5. Add chopped spinach, flavored vinegar and a cup of water.
6. Lock up the lid and cook on HIGH pressure for 10 minutes.
7. Quick-release the pressure.
8. Add ½ cup of water and blend to a paste.
9. Add cashew paste, paneer and Garam Masala and stir thoroughly.
10. Serve over hot rice!

Nutritions: *Calories:367 Fat: 26g Carbohydrates: 21g Protein: 16g Phosphorus: 110mg Potassium: 117mg Sodium: 75mg*

33. BEER PORK RIBS

PREPARATION: 10 MIN

COOKING: 8 H

SERVES: 1

INGREDIENTS

- 2 pounds of pork ribs, cut into two units/racks
- 18 oz. of root beer
- 2 cloves of garlic, minced
- 2 tbsp of onion powder
- 2 tbsp of vegetable oil (optional)

DIRECTIONS

1. Wrap the pork ribs with vegetable oil and place one unit on the bottom of your slow cooker with half of the minced garlic and the onion powder.
2. Place the other rack on top with the rest of the garlic and onion powder.
3. Pour over the root beer and cover the lid.
4. Let simmer for 8 hours on low heat.
5. Take off and finish optionally in a grilling pan for a nice sear.

Nutritions: *Calories: 301 Carbohydrate: 36 g Protein: 21 g Fat: 18 g Sodium: 729 mg Potassium: 200 mg Phosphorus: 209 mg*

34. MEXICAN CHORIZO SAUSAGE

PREPARATION: 10 MIN

COOKING: 15 MIN

SERVES: 1

INGREDIENTS

- 2 pounds of boneless pork but coarsely ground
- 3 tbsp of red wine vinegar
- 2 tbsp of smoked paprika
- ½ tsp of cinnamon
- ½ tsp of ground cloves
- ¼ tsp of coriander seeds
- ¼ tsp ground ginger
- 1 tsp of ground cumin
- 3 tbsp of brandy

DIRECTIONS

1. In a large mixing bowl, combine the ground pork with the seasonings, brandy, and vinegar and mix with your hands well.
2. Place the mixture into a large Ziploc bag and leave in the fridge overnight.
3. Form into 15-16 patties of equal size.
4. Heat the oil in a large pan and fry the patties for 5-7 minutes on each side, or until the meat inside is no longer pink and there is a light brown crust on top.
5. Serve hot.

Nutritions: *Calories: 134 Carbohydrate: 0 g Protein: 10 g Fat: 7 g Sodium: 40 mg Potassium: 138 mg Phosphorus: 128 mg*

35. EGGPLANT CASSEROLE

PREPARATION: 10 MIN   **COOKING: 25-30 MIN**   **SERVES: 4**

INGREDIENTS

- 3 cups of eggplant, peeled and cut into large chunks
- 2 egg whites
- 1 large egg, whole
- ½ cup of unsweetened vegetable
- ¼ tsp of sage
- ½ cup of breadcrumbs
- 1 tbsp of margarine, melted
- 1/4 tsp garlic salt

DIRECTIONS

1. Preheat the oven at 350F/180C.
2. Place the eggplants chunks in a medium pan, cover with a bit of water and cook with the lid covered until tender. Drain from the water and mash with a tool or fork.
3. Beat the eggs with the non-dairy vegetable cream, sage, salt, and pepper. Whisk in the eggplant mush.
4. Combine the melted margarine with the breadcrumbs.
5. Bake in the oven for 20-25 minutes or until the casserole has a golden-brown crust.

Nutritions: *Calories: 186 Carbohydrate: 19 g Protein: 7 g Fat: 9 g Sodium: 503 mg Potassium: 230 mg Phosphorus: 62 mg*

36. CUCUMBER SANDWICH

PREPARATION: 1 H   **COOKING: 5 MIN**   **SERVES: 2**

INGREDIENTS

- 6 tsp. of cream cheese
- 1 pinch of dried dill weed
- 3 tsp. of mayonnaise
- .25 tsp. dry Italian dressing mix
- 4 slices of white bread
- .5 of a cucumber

DIRECTIONS

1. Prepare the cucumber and cut it into slices.
2. Mix cream cheese, mayonnaise, and Italian dressing. Chill for one hour.
3. Distribute the mixture onto the white bread slices.
4. Place cucumber slices on top and sprinkle with the dill weed.
5. Cut in halves and serve.

Nutritions: *Calories: 143 Fat: 6g Carbs: 16.7g Protein: 4g Sodium: 255mg Potassium: 127mg Phosphorus: 64mg*

37. PIZZA PITAS

PREPARATION: 10 MIN

COOKING: 10 MIN

SERVES: 1

INGREDIENTS

- .33 cup of mozzarella cheese
- 2 pieces of pita bread, 6 inches in size
- 6 tsp. of chunky tomato sauce
- 2 cloves of garlic (minced)
- .25 cups of onion, chopped small
- .25 tsp. of red pepper flakes
- .25 cup of bell pepper, chopped small
- 2 ounces of ground pork, lean
- No-stick oil spray
- .5 tsp. of fennel seeds

DIRECTIONS

1. Preheat oven to 400.
2. Put the garlic, ground meat, pepper flakes, onion, and bell pepper in a pan. Sauté until cooked.
3. Grease a flat baking pan and put pitas on it. Use the mixture to spread on the pita bread.
4. Spread one tablespoon of the tomato sauce and top with cheese.
5. Bake for five to eight minutes, until the cheese is bubbling.

Nutritions: *Calories: 284 Fat: 10g Carbs: 34g Protein: 16g Sodium: 795mg Potassium: 706mg Phosphorus: 416mg*

38. LETTUCE WRAPS WITH CHICKEN

PREPARATION: 10 MIN **COOKING: 15 MIN** **SERVES: 4**

INGREDIENTS

- 8 lettuce leaves
- .25 cups of fresh cilantro
- .25 cups of mushroom
- 1 tsp. of five spices seasoning
- .25 cups of onion
- 6 tsp. of rice vinegar
- 2 tsp. of hoisin
- 6 tsp. of oil (canola)
- 3 tsp. of oil (sesame)
- 2 tsp. of garlic
- 2 scallions
- 8 ounces of cooked chicken breast

DIRECTIONS

1. Mince together the cooked chicken and the garlic. Chop up the onions, cilantro, mushrooms, and scallions.
2. Use a skillet overheat, combine chicken to all remaining ingredients, minus the lettuce leaves. Cook for fifteen minutes, stirring occasionally.
3. Place .25 cups of the mixture into each leaf of lettuce.
4. Wrap the lettuce around like a burrito and eat.

Nutritions: *Calories: 84 Fat: 4g Carbs: 9g Protein: 5.9g Sodium: 618mg Potassium: 258mg Phosphorus: 64mg*

39. TURKEY PINWHEELS

PREPARATION: 10 MIN

COOKING: 15 MIN

SERVES: 6

INGREDIENTS

- 6 toothpicks
- 8 oz of spring mix salad greens
- 1 ten-inch tortilla
- 2 ounces of thinly sliced deli turkey
- 9 tsp. of whipped cream cheese
- 1 roasted red bell pepper

DIRECTIONS

1. Cut the red bell pepper into ten strips about a quarter-inch thick.
2. Spread the whipped cream cheese on the tortilla evenly.
3. Add the salad greens to create a base layer and then lay the turkey on top of it.
4. Space out the red bell pepper strips on top of the turkey.
5. Tuck the end and begin rolling the tortilla inward.
6. Use the toothpicks to hold the roll into place and cut it into six pieces.
7. Serve with the swirl facing upward.

Nutritions: *Calories: 206 Fat: 9g Carbs: 21g Protein: 9g Sodium: 533mg Potassium: 145mg Phosphorus: 47mg*

40. CHICKEN TACOS

PREPARATION: 5 MIN

COOKING: 20 MIN

SERVES: 4

INGREDIENTS

- 8 corn tortillas
- 1.5 tsp. of Sodium-free taco seasoning
- 1 juiced lime
- .5 cups of cilantro
- 2 green onions, chopped
- 8 oz of iceberg or romaine lettuce, shredded or chopped
- .25 cup of sour cream
- 1 pound of boneless and skinless chicken breast

DIRECTIONS

1. Cook chicken, by boiling, for twenty minutes. Shred or chop cooked chicken into fine bite-sized pieces.
2. Mix the seasoning and lime juice with the chicken.
3. Put chicken mixture and lettuce in tortillas.
4. Top with the green onions, cilantro, sour cream.

Nutritions: *Calories: 260 Fat: 3g Carbs: 36g Protein: 23g Sodium: 922mg Potassium: 445mg Phosphorus: 357mg*

41. TUNA TWIST

PREPARATION: 10 MIN

COOKING: 30 MIN

SERVES: 4

INGREDIENTS

- 1 can of unsalted or water packaged tuna, drained
- 6 tsp. of vinegar
- .5 cup of cooked peas
- .5 cup celery (chopped)
- 3 tsp. of dried dill weed
- 12 oz cooked macaroni
- .75 cup of mayonnaise

DIRECTIONS

1. Stir together the macaroni, vinegar, and mayonnaise together until blended and smooth.
2. Stir in remaining ingredients.
3. Chill before serving.

Nutritions: *Calories: 290 Fat: 10g Carbs: 32g Protein: 16g Sodium: 307mg Potassium: 175mg Phosphorus: 111mg*

42. CIABATTA ROLLS WITH CHICKEN PESTO

PREPARATION: 10 MIN **COOKING: 20 MIN** **SERVES: 2**

INGREDIENTS

- 6 tsp. of Greek yogurt
- 6 tsp. of pesto
- 2 small ciabatta rolls
- 8 oz of a shredded iceberg or romaine lettuce
- 8 oz of cooked boneless and skinless chicken breast, shredded
- .125 tsp. of pepper

DIRECTIONS

1. Combine the shredded chicken, pesto, pepper, and Greek yogurt in a medium-sized bowl.
2. Slice and toast the ciabatta rolls.
3. Divide the shredded chicken and pesto mixture in half and make sandwiches with the ciabatta rolls.
4. Top with shredded lettuce if desired.

Nutritions: *Calories: 374 Fat: 10g Carbs: 40g Protein: 30g Sodium: 522mg Potassium: 360mg Phosphorus: 84mg*

43. MARINATED SHRIMP PASTA SALAD

PREPARATION: 15 MIN

COOKING: 5 H

SERVES: 1

INGREDIENTS

- 1/4 cup of honey
- 1/4 cup of balsamic vinegar
- 1/2 of an English cucumber, cubed
- 1/2 pound of fully cooked shrimp
- 15 baby carrots
- 1.5 cups of dime-sized cut cauliflower
- 4 stalks of celery, diced
- 1/2 large yellow bell pepper (diced)
- 1/2 red onion (diced)
- 1/2 large red bell pepper (diced)
- 12 ounces of uncooked tri-color pasta (cooked)
- 3/4 cup of olive oil
- 3 tsp. of mustard (Dijon)
- 1/2 tsp. of garlic (powder)
- 1/2 tsp. pepper

DIRECTIONS

1. Cut vegetables and put them in a bowl with the shrimp.
2. Whisk together the honey, balsamic vinegar, garlic powder, pepper, and Dijon mustard in a small bowl. While still whisking, slowly add the oil and whisk it all together.
3. Add the cooled pasta to the bowl with the shrimp and vegetables and mix it.
4. Toss the sauce to coat the pasta, shrimp, and vegetables evenly.
5. Cover and chill for a minimum of five hours before serving. Stir and serve while chilled.

Nutritions: *Calories: 205 Fat: 13g Carbs: 10g Protein: 12g Sodium: 363mg Potassium: 156mg Phosphorus: 109mg*

44. PEANUT BUTTER AND JELLY GRILLED SANDWICH

PREPARATION: 5 MIN

COOKING: 5 MIN

SERVES: 1

INGREDIENTS

- 2 tsp. butter (unsalted)
- 6 tsp. butter (peanut)
- 3 tsp. of flavored jelly
- 2 pieces of bread

DIRECTIONS

1. Put the peanut butter evenly on one bread. Add the layer of jelly.
2. Butter the outside of the pieces of bread.
3. Add the sandwich to a frying pan and toast both sides.

Nutritions: *Calories: 300 Fat: 7g Carbs: 49g Protein: 8g Sodium: 460mg Potassium: 222mg Phosphorus: 80mg*

45. GRILLED ONION AND PEPPER JACK GRILLED CHEESE SANDWICH

PREPARATION: 5 MIN **COOKING: 5 MIN** **SERVES: 2**

INGREDIENTS

- 1 tsp. of oil (olive)
- 6 tsp. of whipped cream cheese
- 1/2 of a medium onion
- 2 ounces of pepper jack cheese
- 4 slices of rye bread
- 2 tsp. of unsalted butter

DIRECTIONS

1. Set out the butter so that it becomes soft. Slice up the onion into thin slices.
2. Sauté onion slices. Continue to stir until cooked. Remove and put it to the side.
3. Spread one tablespoon of the whipped cream cheese on two of the slices of bread.
4. Then add grilled onions and cheese to each slice. Then top using the other two bread slices.
5. Spread the softened butter on the outside of the slices of bread.
6. Use the skillet to toast the sandwiches until lightly brown and the cheese is melted.

Nutritions: *Calories: 350 Fat: 18g Carbs: 34g Protein: 13g Sodium: 589mg Potassium: 184mg Phosphorus: 226mg*

46. GRILLED CORN ON THE COB

PREPARATION: 5 MIN   **COOKING: 20 MIN**   **SERVES: 4**

INGREDIENTS

- 4 frozen corn on the cob, cut in half
- ½ tsp of thyme
- 1 tbsp of grated parmesan cheese
- ¼ tsp of black pepper

DIRECTIONS

1. Combine the oil, cheese, thyme, and black pepper in a bowl.
2. Place the corn in the cheese/oil mix and roll to coat evenly.
3. Fold all 4 pieces in aluminum foil, leaving a small open surface on top.
4. Place the wrapped corns over the grill and let cook for 20 minutes.
5. Serve hot.

Nutritions: *Calories: 125 Carbohydrate: 29.5 g Protein: 2 g Fat: 1.3 g Sodium: 26 g Potassium: 145 mg Phosphorus: 91.5 mg*

CHAPTER 5. DINNER RECIPES

47. GREEN TUNA SALAD

PREPARATION: 10 MIN   **COOKING: 15-20 MIN**   **SERVES: 2**

INGREDIENTS

- 5 ounces of tuna (in freshwater only)
- 2-3 cups of lettuce
- 1/2 cup of Italian tomatoes
- 1 cup of baby marrows
- 1/2 cup of red bell pepper
- 1/4 cup of red onion
- 1/4 cup of fresh thyme
- 2 tbsp olive oil
- 1/8 tsp of black pepper
- 2 tbsp of red wine vinegar

DIRECTIONS

1. Chop the bell pepper, onion, baby marrow, and thyme into small pieces.
2. Add a 3/4 cup of water to a saucepan and add the bell pepper, onion, baby marrow, and thyme to the pan. Let it boil, steam the vegetables by adding a lid on top of the saucepan—steam for 10 minutes.
3. Remove the vegetables and drain them.
4. Combine the vegetables (once cooled down) with the chopped tomatoes and tuna.
5. Mix olive oil, red wine vinegar, and black pepper to create a salad dressing.
6. Add the mixture on a bed of lettuce and drizzle the dressing on top.

Nutritions: *Calories: 210 Fat: 1.5g Carbs: 4g Protein: 43.3g Sodium: 726mg Potassium: 582mg Phosphorus: 296mg*

48. ROASTED CHICKEN AND VEGETABLES

PREPARATION: 10 MIN

COOKING: 45 MIN

SERVES: 2

INGREDIENTS

- 8 oz chicken strips
- 1 ½ cups baby potatoes
- 5 oz green beans
- 2 tbsp sesame seed oil
- 1 tsp of Cajun chicken spice
- ½ tbsp Italian herb dressing

DIRECTIONS

1. Heat the oven to 400 degrees-Fahrenheit
2. Fill up a large pot with water until it is ¾ full. Add the baby potatoes to the pot and cook for 10 minutes.
3. Drain the baby potatoes.
4. Chop off the tips of the green beans.
5. Line a 9 x 13-inch oven tray with parchment paper or spray the oven tray with cooking spray.
6. Place the chicken strips on the tray side, with the green beans and baby potatoes.
7. Add Cajun chicken spice to the chicken breasts and drizzle sesame seed oil over the chicken and vegetables.
8. Roast for 20 minutes.
9. Drizzle Italian herb dressing on top of the chicken and vegetables and roast for another 5-10 minutes.

Nutritions: *Calories: 263 Fat: 6g Sodium: 366mg Potassium: 879mg Phosphorus: 275mg Carbs: 28.6g Protein: 23g*

49. SIRLOIN MEDALLIONS, GREEN SQUASH, AND PINEAPPLE

PREPARATION: 10 MIN

COOKING: 40 MIN

SERVES: 4

INGREDIENTS

- 1 lb. of sirloin medallions
- 1 medium baby marrows
- 1 yellow squash
- ½ onion
- 8 oz of thinly sliced pineapple
- 3 tbsp of olive oil
- 2 tsp of ginger
- ½ tsp of salt
- 1 garlic clove

DIRECTIONS

1. Retrieve thinly sliced pineapple rings from a can and drain. Set the juice aside.
2. Slice garlic and ginger into fine pieces.
3. Mix the pineapple juice, ginger, garlic, salt, and olive oil together in a bowl to create a dressing for the sirloin medallions.
4. Add the sirloin medallions to the marinade and let it sit for 10-15 minutes.
5. Heat the oven to 450 degrees-Fahrenheit and line 2 oven trays with parchment paper.
6. Chop the squash into little ½-inch circles and place it on the parchment paper—drizzle 1tbsp of olive oil on top of it.
7. Cut the onion into small wedges, add to the tray and drizzle with olive oil.
8. Add pineapple rings next to the squash on the first tray and roast for 6 minutes.
9. Remove the pan and turn the squash and pineapple over. Add the onion onto the tray and roast it for another 5 minutes. Close the fruit and vegetables with foil to lock in the heat and set aside.
10. Remove sirloin medallions from the marinade. Line another oven tray pan with parchment paper and place the sirloin medallions on top.
11. Cook for 5 minutes and flip the sirloin to cook for another 5 minutes on the other side.
12. Serve the sirloin medallions with the vegetables and pineapple on a platter.

Nutritions: *Calories: 264 Fat: 12g Carbs: 14g Protein: 25g Sodium: 150mg Potassium: 685mg Phosphorus: 257mg*

50. CHICKEN AND SAVORY RICE

 PREPARATION: 15 MIN

 **COOKING: 45 MIN**

 SERVES: 4

INGREDIENTS

- 4 medium chicken breasts
- 1 baby marrow (chopped)
- 1 red bell pepper (chopped)
- 3 tbsp olive oil
- 1 onion
- 1 garlic clove (minced)
- ½ tsp of black pepper
- 1 tbsp of cumin
- ¼ tsp cayenne pepper
- 2 cups of brown rice

DIRECTIONS

1. Add 2 tbsp of olive oil to medium heat and place the chicken breasts into the pan. Cook for 15 minutes and remove from the pan.
2. Add another tbsp of olive oil to the pan, and add the baby marrow, onion, red pepper, and corn.
3. Sauté the vegetables on medium heat for 10 minutes or until golden brown.
4. Add minced garlic, black pepper, cumin, and cayenne pepper to the vegetables. Stir the vegetables and spices together well.
5. Cut the chicken into cube and add it back to the pan. Mix it with the vegetables for 5 minutes.
6. In a medium pot, fill it up with water until it is 2/3 full. Add the rice to the pot and cook it for 35-40 minutes.
7. Serve the chicken and vegetable mixture on a bed of rice with extra black pepper.

Nutritions: *Calories: 374 Fat: 6.2g Carbs: 65g Protein: 15g Sodium: 520mg Potassium: 645mg Phosphorus: 268mg*

51. SALMON AND GREEN BEANS

PREPARATION: 10 MIN　　**COOKING: 20 MIN**　　**SERVES: 4**

INGREDIENTS

- 3 oz x 4 salmon fillets
- ½ lb. of green beans
- 2 tbsp of dill
- 2 tbsp of coriander
- 2 lemons
- 2 tbsp olive oil
- 4 tbsp of mayonnaise

DIRECTIONS

1. Rinse and salmon fillets and wait for it to dry. Don't remove the skin.
2. Wash green beans and chop the tips of the green beans.
3. Heat the oven up to 425 degrees-Fahrenheit.
4. Spray an oven sheet pan with cooking spray and place the salmon fillets on the sheet pan.
5. Chop up the dill and combine it with the mayonnaise.
6. Put mayo mixture on top of the salmon fillets.
7. Place the green beans next to the salmon fillets and drizzle olive oil on top of everything.
8. Place the oven baking sheet in the middle of the oven and cook for 15 minutes.
9. Slice the lemons into wedges and serve with the salmon fillets and green beans.

Nutritions: *Calories: 399 Fat: 21g Carbs: 8g Protein: 38g Sodium: 229mg Potassium: 1000mg Phosphorus: 723mg*

52. BAKED MACARONI & CHEESE

PREPARATION: 10 MIN

COOKING: 40-45 MIN

SERVES: 1

INGREDIENTS

- 3 cups of macaroni
- 2 cups of milk
- 2 tbsp of butter (unsalted)
- 2 tbsp of flour (all-purpose)
- 2 ½ cups of cheddar
- 2 tbsp of blanched almonds
- 1 tbsp of thyme
- 1 tbsp of olive oil
- 1 cheese sauce (quick make packets)

DIRECTIONS

1. Preheat the oven to 350 degrees-Fahrenheit.
2. Prepare a medium-sized pot on the stove and fill it up with water.
3. Add the macaroni to the pot with a tbsp of olive oil for 8-10 minutes. Stir until cooked.
4. In a measuring cup, measure your butter and flour and mix it. Place it in the microwave for 1 minute. Then stir in the milk, spices, and herbs—microwave for 2-3 minutes, or until the mixture is thick.
5. Drain the noodles and add to a casserole dish that has been sprayed with cooking spray, the sauce, and cheese. Mix it well, followed with more cheese on top.
6. Put and bake casserole dish into the oven for 15-20 minutes.
7. Serve with blanched almonds on top.

Nutritions: *Calories: 314 Fat: 14g Carbs: 34g Protein: 19g Sodium: 373mg Potassium: 120mg Phosphorus: 222mg*

53. KOREAN PEAR SALAD

PREPARATION: 5 MIN

COOKING: 15 MIN

SERVES: 2

INGREDIENTS

- 6 cups green lettuce
- 4 medium-sized pears (peeled, cored, and diced)
- ½ cup of sugar
- ½ cup of pecan nuts
- ½ cup of water
- 2 oz of blue cheese
- ½ cup of cranberries
- ½ cup of dressing

DIRECTIONS

1. Dissolve the water and sugar in a frying pan (non-stick).
2. Heat the mixture until it turns into a syrup, and then add the nuts immediately.
3. Place the syrup with the nuts on a piece of parchment paper and separate the nuts while the mixture is hot. Let it cool down.
4. Prepare lettuce in a salad bowl and add the pears, blue cheese, and cranberries to the salad.
5. Add the caramelized nuts to the salad and serve it with a dressing of choice on the side.

Nutritions: *Calories: 112 Fat: 9g Carbs: 5.5g Protein: 2g Sodium: 130mg Potassium: 160mg Phosphorus: 71.7mg*

54. BEEF ENCHILADAS

PREPARATION: 10 MIN

COOKING: 30 MIN

SERVES: 1

INGREDIENTS

- 1 pound of lean beef
- 12 whole-wheat tortillas
- 1 can of low-sodium enchilada sauce
- ½ cup of onion (diced)
- ½ tsp of black pepper
- 1 garlic clove
- 1 tbsp of olive oil
- 1 tsp of cumin

DIRECTIONS

1. Heat the oven to 375 degrees-Fahrenheit
2. In a medium-sized frying pan, cook the beef in olive oil until completely cooked.
3. Add the minced garlic, diced onion, cumin, and black pepper to the pan and mix everything in with the beef.
4. In a separate pan, cook the tortillas in olive oil and dip each cooked tortilla in the enchilada sauce.
5. Fill the tortilla with the meat mixture and roll it up.
6. Put the finished product in a slightly heated pan with cheese on top.
7. Bake the tortillas in the pan until crispy, golden brown, and the cheese is melted.

Nutritions: *Calories: 177 Fat: 6g Carbs: 15g Protein: 15g Sodium: 501mg Potassium: 231mg Phosphorus: 98mg*

55. CHICKEN AND BROCCOLI CASSEROLE

PREPARATION: 15 MIN

COOKING: 45 MIN - 1 H

SERVES: 1

INGREDIENTS

- 2 cups of rice (cooked)
- 3 chicken breasts
- 2 cups of broccoli
- 1 onion (diced)
- 2 eggs
- 2 cups of cheddar cheese
- 2 tbsp of butter
- 1-2 tbsp of parmesan cheese

DIRECTIONS

1. Heat the oven to 350 degrees-Fahrenheit
2. Add the broccoli to a bowl and cover it with plastic wrap. Microwave the broccoli for 2-3 minutes.
3. Dice the onion and add it with the chicken and the butter in the pa.
4. Cook the chicken for 15 minutes.
5. Once the chicken is cooked, mix it, broccoli, and rice together, and add to a greased casserole dish.
6. Add the grated cheese into the casserole dish and stir well.
7. Add the parmesan cheese on top.
8. Place the casserole dish in the oven for 30-45 minutes.

Nutritions: *Calories: 349 Fat: 12g Carbs: 14g Protein: 44g Sodium: 980mg Potassium: 713mg Phosphorus: 451mg*

56. PUMPKIN BITES

PREPARATION: 10 MIN

COOKING: 5 MIN

SERVES: 12

INGREDIENTS

- 8 oz cream cheese
- 1 tsp vanilla
- 1 tsp pumpkin pie spice
- 1/4 cup coconut flour
- 1/4 cup erythritol
- 1/2 cup pumpkin puree
- 4 oz butter

DIRECTIONS

1. Add all ingredients into the mixing bowl and beat using hand mixer until well combined.
2. Scoop mixture into the silicone ice cube tray and place it in the refrigerator until set.
3. Serve and enjoy.

Nutritions: *Calories 149 Fat 14.6 g Carbohydrates 8.1 g Sugar 5.4 g Protein 2 g Cholesterol 41 mg Phosphorus: 66mg Potassium: 77mg Sodium: 55mg*

CHAPTER 6. POULTRY MAINS RECIPES

57. CHICKEN CURRY

PREPARATION: 10 MIN

COOKING: 4 MIN

SERVES: 4

INGREDIENTS

- 1lb skinless chicken breasts
- 1 medium onion, thinly sliced
- 1 15 ounce can chickpeas, drained and rinsed well
- 2 medium sweet potatoes, peeled and diced
- ½ cup light coconut milk
- ½ cup chicken stock (see recipe)
- 1 15ounce can sodium-free tomato sauce
- 2 tablespoon curry powder
- 1 teaspoon low-sodium salt
- ½ cayenne powder
- 1 cup green peas
- 2 tablespoon lemon juice

DIRECTIONS

1. Place the chicken breasts, onion, chickpeas, and sweet potatoes into a 4 to 6-quart slow cooker.
2. Mix the coconut milk, chicken stock, tomato sauce, curry powder, salt, and cayenne together and pour into the slow cooker, stirring to coat well.
3. Cover and cook on low for 8 hours or high for 4 hours.
4. Stir in the peas and lemon juice 5 minutes before serving.

Nutritions: *Calories 302, Fat 5g, Carbs 43g, Protein 24g, Fiber 9g, Potassium 573mg, Sodium 800mg*

58. LEMON & HERB TURKEY BREASTS

PREPARATION: 25 MIN

COOKING: 3 1/2 H

SERVES: 12

INGREDIENTS

- 1 can (14-1/2 ounces) chicken broth
- 1/2 cup lemon juice
- 1/4 cup packed brown sugar
- 1/4 cup fresh sage
- 1/4 cup fresh thyme leaves
- 1/4 cup lime juice
- 1/4 cup cider vinegar
- 1/4 cup olive oil
- 1 envelope low-sodium onion soup mix
- 2 tablespoon dijon mustard
- 1 tablespoon fresh marjoram, minced
- 1 teaspoon paprika
- 1 teaspoon garlic powder
- 1 teaspoon pepper
- ½ teaspoon low-sodium salt
- 2 2lb boneless skinless turkey breast halves

DIRECTIONS

1. Make a marinade by blending all the ingredients in a blender.
2. Pour over the turkey and leave overnight.
3. Place the turkey and marinade in a 4 to 6-quart slow cooker and cover.
4. Cover and cook on high for 3-1/2 to 4-1/2 hours or until a thermometer reads 165°.

Nutritions: *Calories 219, Fat 5g, Carbs 3g, Protein 36g, Fiber 0g, Potassium 576mg, Sodium 484mg*

59. BEEF CHIMICHANGAS

PREPARATION: 10 MIN

COOKING: 10-12 H

SERVES: 16

INGREDIENTS

- Shredded beef
- 3lb boneless beef chuck roast, fat trimmed away
- 3 tablespoon low-sodium taco seasoning mix
- 1 10ounce canned low-sodium diced tomatoes
- 6ounce canned diced green chilies with the juice
- 3 garlic cloves, minced
- To serve
- 16 medium flour tortillas
- Sodium-free refried beans
- Mexican rice, sour cream, cheddar cheese
- Guacamole, salsa, lettuce

DIRECTIONS

1. Arrange the beef in a 5-quart or larger slow cooker.
2. Sprinkle over taco seasoning and coat well.
3. Add tomatoes and garlic and cover.
4. Cook on low for 10 to 12 hours.
5. When cooked remove the beef and shred.
6. Make burritos out of the shredded beef, refried beans, mexican rice, and cheese.
7. Bake for 10 minutes at 350° f until brown.
8. Serve with salsa, lettuce, and guacamole.

Nutritions: *Calories 249, Fat 18g, Carbs 3g, Protein 33g, Fiber 5g, Potassium 633mg, Sodium 457mg*

60. MEAT LOAF

 PREPARATION: 5 MIN

 COOKING: 5-6 H

 SERVES: 6

INGREDIENTS

- 2-pound lean ground beef
- 2 whole eggs, beaten
- ¾ cup milk
- ¾ cup breadcrumbs
- ½ cup chicken broth (see recipe)
- ¼ cup onion, finely diced
- 3 garlic cloves, minced
- 1 teaspoon low-sodium salt
- ¼ teaspoon freshly ground black pepper
- ¼ cup low sodium chili sauce
- Nonstick spray

DIRECTIONS

1. Mix the beaten eggs, milk, oatmeal, spices, onion, garlic, and chicken broth until well combined.
2. Mix in the beef and place in a 5-quart or larger slow cooker, sprayed with nonstick spray.
3. Cover and cook on low for 5 to 6 hours.
4. Serve with low-sodium ketchup.

Nutritions: *Calories 280, Fat 10g, Carbs 9g, Protein 37g, Fiber 1g, Potassium 648mg, Sodium 325mg*

61. CROCKPOT PEACHY PORK CHOPS

PREPARATION: 30 MIN   COOKING: 2-3 H   SERVES: 8

INGREDIENTS

- 4 large peaches, pitted and peeled
- 1 onion, finely minced
- ¼ cup ketchup
- ¼ cup low-sodium honey barbecue sauce
- 2 tablespoon brown sugar
- 1 tablespoon low sodium soy sauce
- ¼ teaspoon low-sodium garlic salt
- ½ teaspoon ground ginger
- 2lb boneless pork chops
- 3 tablespoon olive oil

DIRECTIONS

1. Puree the peaches with a blender.
2. Mix the peach puree with the onion, ketchup, barbecue sauce, brown sugar, soy sauce, salt, garlic salt, and ginger.
3. Brown the pork chops in a large skillet then transfer to a 6-quart or larger slow cooker.
4. Pour the sauce over the pork chops and cover.
5. Cook for 5 to 6 hours on high.

Nutritions: *Calories 252, Fat 8g, Carbs 18g, Protein 26g, Fiber 1g, Potassium 710mg, Sodium 325mg*

62. CHICKEN AVOCADO SALAD

PREPARATION: 8 MIN   **COOKING: 20 MIN**   **SERVES: 8**

INGREDIENTS

- 3 avocados - peeled, pitted and diced
- 1-pound grilled skinless, boneless chicken breast, diced
- 1/2cupfinely chopped red onion
- 1/2cupchopped fresh cilantro
- 1/4cupbalsamic vinaigrette salad dressing

DIRECTIONS

1. Mix together the chicken, avocados, cilantro, and onion in a medium-sized bowl. Pour over the balsamic vinaigrette dressing. Toss lightly to coat all the ingredients.

Nutritions: *Calories: 252 Total Fat: 17.5g Carbohydrates: 8.3g Protein: 17.2g Cholesterol: 43 Mg Sodium: 130 Mg*

63. CHICKEN MANGO SALSA SALAD WITH CHIPOTLE LIME VINAIGRETTE

PREPARATION: 30 MIN

COOKING: 30 MIN

SERVES: 6

INGREDIENTS

- 1 mango - peeled, seeded and diced
- 2 roam (plum) tomatoes, chopped
- 1/2 onion, chopped
- 1 jalapeno pepper, seeded and chopped - or to taste
- 1/4cupcilantro leaves, chopped
- 1 lime, juiced
- 1/2cupolive oil
- 1/4cuplime juice
- 1/4cupwhite sugar
- 1/2 teaspoon ground chipotle chile powder
- 1/2 teaspoon ground cumin
- 1/4 teaspoon garlic powder
- 1 (10 ounce) bag baby spinach leaves
- 1cupbroccoli coleslaw mix
- 1cupdiced cooked chicken
- 3 tablespoons. Diced red bell pepper
- 3 tablespoons. Diced green bell pepper
- 2 tablespoons. Diced yellow bell pepper
- 2 tablespoons. Dried cranberries
- 2 tablespoons. Chopped pecans
- 2 tablespoons. Crumbled blue cheese

DIRECTIONS

1. In a big bowl, combine the jalapeno pepper, juiced lime, mango, cilantro, tomatoes, and onion. Set the mixture aside.
2. In a separate bowl, whisk together the garlic powder, olive oil, cumin, a quarters lime juice, chipotle, and sugar. Set the mixture aside.
3. In another big bowl, toss together the cranberries, spinach, broccoli coleslaw mix, pecans, chicken, and yellow, green and red bell peppers.
4. Top with blue cheese and mango salsa. Make sure they're spread all over.
5. Drizzle the dressing over salad. Toss to serve.

Nutritions: *Calories: 317 Total Fat: 22.3g Carbohydrates: 25g Protein: 7.6g Cholesterol: 14mg Sodium: 110mg*

64. CHICKEN SALAD BALSAMIC

PREPARATION: 15 MIN **COOKING: 15 MIN** **SERVES: 6**

INGREDIENTS

- 3 cup diced cold, cooked chicken
- 1 cup diced apple
- 1/2 cup diced celery
- 2 green onions, chopped
- 1/2 cup chopped walnuts
- 3 tablespoons. Balsamic vinegar
- 5 tablespoons. Olive oil
- Salt and pepper to taste

DIRECTIONS

1. Toss together the celery, chicken, onion, walnuts, and apple in a big bowl.
2. Whisk the oil together with the vinegar in a small bowl. Pour the dressing over the salad. Then add pepper and salt to taste. Combine the ingredients thoroughly. Leave the mixture for 10-15 minutes. Toss once more and chill.

Nutritions: *Calories: 336 Total Fat: 26.8g Carbohydrates: 6g Protein: 19g Cholesterol: 55mg Sodium: 58mg*

65. CHICKEN SALAD WITH APPLES, GRAPES, AND WALNUTS

PREPARATION: 25 MIN

COOKING: 25 MIN

SERVES: 12

INGREDIENTS

- 4 cooked chicken breasts, shredded
- 2 granny smith apples, cut into small chunks
- 2cupchopped walnuts, or to taste
- 1/2 red onion, chopped
- 3 stalks celery, chopped
- 3 tablespoons. Lemon juice
- 1/2cupvanilla yogurt
- 5 tablespoons. Creamy salad dressing (such as miracle whip®)
- 5 tablespoons. Mayonnaise
- 25 seedless red grapes, halved

DIRECTIONS

1. In a big bowl, toss together the shredded chicken, lemon juice, apple chunks, celery, red onion, and walnuts.
2. Get another bowl and whisk together the dressing, vanilla yogurt, and mayonnaise. Pour over the chicken mixture. Toss to coat. Fold the grapes carefully into the salad.

Nutritions: *Calories: 307 Total Fat: 22.7g Carbohydrates: 10.8g Protein: 17.3g Cholesterol: 41mg Sodium: 128mg*

66. CHICKEN STRAWBERRY SPINACH SALAD WITH GINGER-LIME DRESSING

PREPARATION: 10 MIN

COOKING: 30 MIN

SERVES: 2

INGREDIENTS

- 2 teaspoons. Corn oil
- 1 skinless, boneless chicken breast half - cut into bite-size pieces
- 1/2 teaspoon garlic powder
- 1 1/2 tablespoons. Mayonnaise
- 1/2 lime, juiced
- 1/2 teaspoon ground ginger
- 2 teaspoons. Milk
- 2cupfresh spinach, stems removed
- 4 fresh strawberries, sliced
- 1 1/2 tablespoons. Slivered almonds
- Freshly ground black pepper to taste

DIRECTIONS

1. In a skillet, heat oil over medium heat. Add the chicken breast and garlic powder. Cook the chicken for 10 minutes per side. When the juices run clear, remove from heat and set aside.
2. Combine the lime juice, milk, mayonnaise, and ginger in a bowl.
3. Place the spinach on serving dishes. Top with strawberries and chicken. Then sprinkle with almonds. Drizzle the salad with the dressing. Add pepper and serve.

Nutritions: *Calories: 242 Total Fat: 17.3g Carbohydrates: 7.5g Protein: 15.8g Cholesterol: 40mg Sodium: 117mg*

67. ASIAN CHICKEN SATAY

PREPARATION: 15 MIN

COOKING: 10 MIN

SERVES: 6

INGREDIENTS

- Juice of 2 limes
- Brown sugar – 2 tablespoons
- Minced garlic – 1 tablespoon
- Ground cumin – 2 teaspoons
- Boneless, skinless chicken breast – 12, cut into strips

DIRECTIONS

1. In a bowl, stir together the cumin, garlic, brown sugar, and lime juice.
2. Add the chicken strips to the bowl and marinate in the refrigerator for 1 hour.
3. Heat the barbecue to medium-high.
4. Remove the chicken from the marinade and thread each strip onto wooden skewers that have been soaked in the water.
5. Grill the chicken for about 4 minutes per side or until the meat is cooked through but still juicy.

Nutritions: *Calories: 78 Carb: 4g Phosphorus: 116mg Potassium: 108mg Sodium: 100mg Protein: 12g*

68. ZUCCHINI AND TURKEY BURGER WITH JALAPENO PEPPERS

PREPARATION: 15 MIN

COOKING: 10 MIN

SERVES: 4

INGREDIENTS

- Turkey meat (ground) – 1 pound
- Zucchini (shredded) – 1 cup
- Onion (minced) – ½ cup
- Jalapeño pepper (seeded and minced) – 1
- Egg – 1
- Extra-spicy blend – 1 teaspoon
- Fresh poblano peppers (seeded and sliced in half lengthwise)
- Mustard – 1 teaspoon

DIRECTIONS

1. Start by taking a mixing bowl and adding in the turkey meat, zucchini, onion, jalapeño pepper, egg, and extra-spicy blend. Mix well to combine.
2. Divide the mixture into 4 equal portions. Form burger patties out of the same.
3. Prepare an electric griddle or an outdoor grill. Place the burger patties on the grill and cook until the top is blistered and tender. Place the sliced poblano peppers on the grill alongside the patties. Grilling the patties should take about 5 minutes on each side.
4. Once done, place the patties onto the buns and top them with grilled peppers.

Nutritions: *Protein 25g Carbohydrates 5g Fat 10g Cholesterol 125mg Sodium 128 Mg Potassium 475mg Phosphorus 280mg Calcium 43mg Fiber 1.6g*

69. GNOCCHI AND CHICKEN DUMPLINGS

PREPARATION: 10 MIN **COOKING: 40 MIN** **SERVES: 10**

INGREDIENTS

- Chicken breast – 2 pounds
- Gnocchi – 1 pound
- Light olive oil – ¼ cup
- Better than bouillon® chicken base – 1 tablespoon
- Chicken stock (reduced-sodium) – 6 cups
- Fresh celery (diced finely) – ½ cup
- Fresh onions (diced finely) – ½ cup
- Fresh carrots (diced finely) – ½ cup
- Fresh parsley (chopped) – ¼ cup
- Black pepper – 1 teaspoon
- Italian seasoning – 1 teaspoon

DIRECTIONS

1. Start by placing the stock over a high flame. Add in the oil and let it heat through.
2. Add the chicken to the hot oil and shallow-fry until all sides turn golden brown.
3. Toss in the carrots, onions, and celery and cook for about 5 minutes. Pour in the chicken stock and let it cool on a high flame for about 30 minutes.
4. Reduce the flame and add in the chicken bouillon, italian seasoning, and black pepper. Stir well.
5. Toss in the store-bought gnocchi and let it cook for about 15 minutes. Keep stirring.
6. Once done, transfer into a serving bowl. Add parsley and serve hot!

Nutritions: *Protein 28g Carbohydrates 38g Fat 10g Cholesterol 58mg Sodium 121mg Potassium 485mg Calcium 38mg Fiber 2g*

CHAPTER 7. MEAT RECIPES

70. PEPPERCORN PORK CHOPS

PREPARATION: 30 MIN   **COOKING: 30 MIN**   **SERVES: 4**

INGREDIENTS

- 1 tablespoon crushed black peppercorns
- 4 pork loin chops
- 2 tablespoons olive oil
- 1/4 cup butter
- 5 garlic cloves
- 1 cup green and red bell peppers
- 1/2 cup pineapple juice

DIRECTIONS

1. Sprinkle and press peppercorns into both sides of pork chops.
2. Heat oil, butter and garlic cloves in a large skillet over medium heat, stirring frequently.
3. Add pork chops and cook uncovered for 5–6 minutes.
4. Dice the bell peppers. Add the bell peppers and pineapple juice to the pork chops.
5. Cover and simmer for another 5–6 minutes or until pork is thoroughly cooked.

Nutritions: *Calories 317, Total Fat 25.7g, Saturated Fat 10.5g, Cholesterol 66mg, Sodium 126mg, Total Carbohydrate 9.2g, Dietary Fiber 2g, Total Sugars 6.4g, Protein 13.2g, Calcium 39mg, Iron 1mg, Potassium 250mg, Phosphorus 115 mg*

71. PORK CHOPS WITH APPLES, ONIONS

PREPARATION: 30 MIN

COOKING: 1 H

SERVES: 4

INGREDIENTS

- 4 pork chops
- salt and pepper to taste
- 2 onions, sliced into rings
- 2 apples - peeled, cored, and sliced into rings
- 3 tablespoons honey
- 2 teaspoons freshly ground black pepper

DIRECTIONS

1. Preheat oven to 375 degrees F.
2. Season pork chops with salt and pepper to taste, and arrange in a medium oven-safe skillet. Top pork chops with onions and apples. Sprinkle with honey. Season with 2 teaspoons pepper.
3. Cover, and bake 1 hour in the preheated oven, pork chops have reached an internal temperature of 145 degrees F.

Nutritions: *Calories 307, Total Fat 16.1g, Saturated Fat 6g, Cholesterol 55mg, Sodium 48mg, Total Carbohydrate 26.8g, Dietary Fiber 3.1g, Total Sugars 21.5g, Protein 15.1g, Calcium 30mg, Iron 1mg, Potassium 387mg, Phosphorus 315 mg*

72. BAKED LAMB CHOPS

PREPARATION: 10 MIN

COOKING: 45 MIN

SERVES: 4

INGREDIENTS

- 2 eggs
- 2 teaspoons Worcestershire sauce
- 8 (5.5 ounces) lamb chops
- 2 cups graham crackers

DIRECTIONS

1. Preheat oven to 375 degrees F.
2. In a medium bowl, combine the eggs and the Worcestershire sauce; stir well. Dip each lamb chop in the sauce and then lightly dredge in the graham crackers. Then arrange them in a 9x13-inch baking dish.
3. Bake at 375 degrees F for 20 minutes, turn chops over and cook for 20 more minutes, or to the desired doneness.

Nutritions: *Calories176, Total Fat 5.7g, Saturated Fat 1.4g, Cholesterol 72mg, Sodium 223mg, Total Carbohydrate 21.9g, Dietary Fiber 0.8g, Total Sugars 9.2g, Protein 9.1g, Vitamin D 5mcg, Calcium 17mg, Iron 2mg, Potassium 121mg, Phosphorus 85 mg*

73. GRILLED LAMB CHOPS WITH PINEAPPLE

PREPARATION: 15 MIN

COOKING: 55 MIN

SERVES: 4

INGREDIENTS

- 1 lemon, zest and juiced
- 2 tablespoons chopped fresh oregano
- 2 cloves garlic, minced
- salt and black pepper to taste
- 8 (3 ounces) lamb chops
- 1/2 cup fresh unsweetened pineapple juice
- 1 cup pineapples

DIRECTIONS

1. Whisk together the lemon zest and juice, oregano, garlic, salt, and black pepper in a bowl; pour into a resealable plastic bag. Add the lamb chops, coat with the marinade, squeeze out excess air, and seal the bag.
2. Set aside to marinate.
3. Preheat an outdoor grill for medium-high heat, and lightly oil the grate.
4. Bring the pineapple juice in a small saucepan over high heat.
5. Reduce heat to medium-low, and continue simmering until the liquid has reduced to half of its original volume, about 45 minutes.
6. Stir in the pineapples and set aside.
7. Remove the lamb from the marinade and shake off excess.
8. Discard the remaining marinade.
9. Cook the chops on the preheated grill until they start to firm and are reddish-pink and juicy in the center, about 4 minutes per side for medium rare.
10. Serve the chops drizzled with the pineapple reduction.

Nutritions: *Calories 69, Total Fat 1.6g, Saturated Fat 0.5g, Cholesterol 17mg, Sodium 16mg, Total Carbohydrate 8.5g, Dietary Fiber 1.4g, Total Sugars 5.1g, Protein 5.9g, Calcium 37mg, Iron 1mg, Potassium 163mg, Phosphorus 65 mg*

74. LEMON AND THYME LAMB CHOPS

PREPARATION: 10 MIN

COOKING: 10 MIN

SERVES: 4

INGREDIENTS

- 1 tablespoon olive oil
- 1/4 tablespoon lemon juice
- 1 tablespoon chopped fresh thyme
- Salt and pepper to taste
- 4 lamb chops

DIRECTIONS

1. Stir together olive oil, lemon juice, and thyme in a small bowl. Season with salt and pepper to taste. Place lamb chops in a shallow dish and brush with the olive oil mixture. Marinate in the refrigerator for 1 hour.
2. Preheat grill for high heat.
3. Lightly oil grill grate. Place lamb chops on the grill, and discard marinade. Cook for 10 minutes, turning once, or to the desired doneness

Nutritions: *Calories 111, Total Fat 6.7g, Saturated Fat 1.6g, Cholesterol 38mg, Sodium 33mg, Total Carbohydrate 0.5g, Dietary Fiber 0.3g, Total Sugars 0g, Protein 12g, Calcium 19mg, Iron 2mg, Potassium 149mg, Phosphorus 93mg*

75. BASIL GRILLED MEDITERRANEAN LAMB CHOPS

PREPARATION: 10 MIN

COOKING: 10 MIN

SERVES: 4

INGREDIENTS

- 4 (8 ounces) lamb shoulder chops
- 2 tablespoons Dijon mustard
- 2 tablespoons balsamic vinegar
- ½ tablespoon garlic powder
- 1/4 teaspoon ground black pepper
- 1/2 cup olive oil
- 2 tablespoons shredded fresh basil, or to taste

DIRECTIONS

1. Pat lamb chops dry and arrange in a single layer in a shallow glass baking dish.
2. Whisk Dijon mustard, balsamic vinegar, garlic, and pepper together in a small bowl.
3. Whisk in oil slowly until marinade is smooth.
4. Stir in basil. Pour marinade over lamb chops, turning to coat both sides.
5. Cover and refrigerate for 1 to 4 hours.
6. Bring lamb chops to room temperature, about 30 minutes.
7. Preheat grill for medium heat and lightly oil the grate.
8. Grill lamb chops until browned, 5 to 10 minutes per side.
9. An instant-read thermometer inserted into the center should read at least 145 degrees F.

Nutritions: *Calories 270, Total Fat 27.8g, Saturated Fat 4.4g, Cholesterol 19mg, Sodium 109mg, Total Carbohydrate 1.4g, Dietary Fiber 0.4g, Total Sugars 0.4g, Protein 6.1g, Calcium 14mg, Iron 1mg, Potassium 33mg, Phosphorus 30mg*

76. SHREDDED BEEF

PREPARATION: 10 MIN   **COOKING: 5 H 10 MIN**   **SERVES: 4**

INGREDIENTS

- 1/2 cup onion
- 2 garlic cloves
- 2 tablespoons fresh parsley
- 2-pound beef rump roast
- 1 tablespoon Italian herb seasoning
- 1 teaspoon dried parsley
- 1 bay leaf
- 1/2 teaspoon pepper
- 1/4 teaspoon salt
- 2 tablespoons olive oil
- 1/3 cup vinegar
- 2 to 3 cups water
- 8 hard rolls, 3-1/2-inch diameter, 2 ounces each

DIRECTIONS

1. Chop onion, garlic and fresh parsley. Place beef roast in a Crock-Pot. Add chopped onion, garlic and remaining ingredients, except fresh parsley and rolls, to Crock-Pot; stir to combine.
2. Cover and cook on low-heat setting for 8 to 10 hours, or on high setting for 4 to 5 hours, until fork-tender.
3. Remove roast from Crock-Pot.
4. Shred with two forks then return meat to cooking broth to keep warm until ready to serve.
5. Slice rolls in half and top with shredded beef, fresh parsley and 1-2 spoons of the broth.
6. Serve open-face or as a sandwich.

Nutritions: *Calories 218, Total Fat 9.7g, Saturated Fat 2.6g, Cholesterol 75mg, Sodium 184mg, Total Carbohydrate 5.1g, Dietary Fiber 0.4g, Total Sugars 0.4g, Protein 26g, Calcium 26mg, Iron 3mg, Potassium 28mg, Phosphorus 30mg*

77. LAMB STEW WITH GREEN BEANS

PREPARATION: 30 MIN

COOKING: 1 H 10 MIN

SERVES: 4

INGREDIENTS

- 1 tablespoon olive oil
- 1 large onion, chopped
- 1 stalk green onion, chopped
- 1-pound boneless lamb shoulder, cut into 2-inch pieces
- 3 cups hot water
- ½ pound fresh green beans, trimmed
- 1 tablespoon chopped fresh parsley
- 1/2 teaspoon dried mint
- 1/2 teaspoon dried dill weed
- 1 pinch ground nutmeg
- ¼ teaspoon honey
- Salt and pepper to taste

DIRECTIONS

1. Heat oil in a large pot over medium heat. Saute onion and green onion until golden.
2. Stir in lamb, and cook until evenly brown.
3. Stir in water. Reduce heat and simmer for about 1 hour.
4. Stir in green beans. Season with parsley, mint, dill, nutmeg, honey, salt and pepper.
5. Continue cooking until beans are tender.

Nutritions: *Calories 81, Total Fat 5.1g, Saturated Fat 1.1g, Cholesterol 19mg, Sodium 20mg, Total Carbohydrate 2.8g, Dietary Fiber 1g, Total Sugars 1g, Protein 6.5g, Calcium 17mg, Iron 1mg, Potassium 136mg, Phosphorus 120mg*

78. GRILLED LAMB CHOPS WITH FRESH MINT

PREPARATION: 15 MIN

COOKING: 10 MIN

SERVES: 4

INGREDIENTS

- 8 (5 ounces) lamb loin chops, about 1 1/4-inches thick
- 1/8 teaspoon seasoning salt
- 1/2 tablespoon dried parsley
- 1/2 tablespoon minced fresh mint
- 1/2 tablespoon dried rosemary

DIRECTIONS

1. Trim any excess fat down to 1/8-inch around each lamb chop and sprinkle both sides with seasoning salt.
2. Let sit for about 30 minutes to come to room temperature.
3. Preheat an outdoor grill to 400 degrees F. Lightly oil the grate once the grill is hot.
4. Place lamb chops on the hot grate and grill for 2 to 3 minutes.
5. Rotate chops, to achieve crisscross grill marks, and continue grilling, 2 to 3 more minutes.
6. Flip the chops and grill for 2 to 3 minutes.
7. Rotate chops and continue grilling an additional 2 minutes, or until they have reached the desired doneness.
8. An instant-read thermometer inserted into the center should read at least 130 degrees F.
9. Remove chops from grill and sprinkle with dried herbs and fresh mint.
10. Allow to rest under the foil, about 10 minutes

Nutritions: *Calories 160, Total Fat 6.3g, Saturated Fat 2.3g, Cholesterol 77mg, Sodium 139mg, Total Carbohydrate 0.4g, Dietary Fiber 0.2g, Total Sugars 0g, Protein 23.9g, Calcium 18mg, Iron 2mg, Potassium 295mg, Phosphorus 140mg*

79. LAMB KEEMA

PREPARATION: 5 MIN

COOKING: 20 MIN

SERVES: 4

INGREDIENTS

- 1 1/2 pounds ground lamb
- 1 onion, finely chopped
- 2 teaspoons garlic powder
- 2 tablespoons garam masala
- 1/8 teaspoon salt
- 3/4 cup chicken broth

DIRECTIONS

1. In a large, heavy skillet over medium heat, cook ground lamb until evenly brown.
2. While cooking, break apart with a wooden spoon until crumbled.
3. Transfer cooked lamb to a bowl and drain off all but 1 tablespoon fat. Saute onion until soft and translucent, about 5 minutes.
4. Stir in garlic powder, and sauté 1 minute.
5. Stir in garam masala and cook 1 minute.
6. Return the browned lamb to the pan, and stir in chicken beef broth.
7. Reduce heat, and simmer for 10 to 15 minutes or until meat is fully cooked through, and liquid has evaporated.

Nutritions: *Calories 194, Total Fat 7.3g, Saturated Fat 2.6g, Cholesterol 87mg, Sodium 160mg, Total Carbohydrate 2.2g, Dietary Fiber 0.4g, Total Sugars 0.9g, Protein 28.1g, Calcium 18mg, Iron 2mg, Potassium 379mg, Phosphorus 240mg*

80. CURRY LAMB BALLS

PREPARATION: 15 MIN   **COOKING: 15 MIN**   **SERVES: 4**

INGREDIENTS

- ½-pound ground lamb
- 1/2 cup graham crackers
- Dried basil to taste
- 1 (10 ounces) can soy milk
- 1 1/2 tablespoons green curry paste

DIRECTIONS

1. In a medium bowl, mix together the ground lamb, graham crackers and basil until well blended.
2. Form into meatballs about 1 inch in diameter.
3. Heat a greased skillet over medium-high heat and fry the lamb balls until they are a bit black and crusty, about 5 minutes.
4. Remove balls from pan and set aside.
5. Toss the curry paste into the hot skillet and fry for about a minute.
6. Then pour in the entire can of soy milk and lower the heat.
7. Let the mixture simmer, frequently stirring for 5 to 10 minutes.
8. Serve.

Nutritions: *Calories 103, Total Fat 3.8g, Saturated Fat 0.9g, Cholesterol 26mg, Sodium 184mg, Total Carbohydrate 7.1g, Dietary Fiber 0.4g, Total Sugars 3g, Protein 9.5g, Calcium 14mg, Iron 1mg, Potassium 144mg, Phosphorus 90mg*

81. SPICED LAMB BURGERS

PREPARATION: 10 MIN **COOKING: 20 MIN** **SERVES: 2**

INGREDIENTS

- 1 tablespoon extra-virgin olive oil
- 1 teaspoon cumin
- ½ finely diced red onion
- 1 minced garlic clove
- 1 teaspoon harissa spices
- 1 cup arugula
- 1 juiced lemon
- 6-ounce lean ground lamb
- 1 tablespoon parsley
- ½ cup low-fat plain yogurt

DIRECTIONS

1. Preheat the broiler on a medium to high heat.
2. Mix together the ground lamb, red onion, parsley, harissa spices and olive oil until combined.
3. Shape 1-inch thick patties using wet hands.
4. Add the patties to a baking tray and place under the broiler for 7-8 minutes on each side or until thoroughly cooked through.
5. Mix the yogurt, lemon juice and cumin and serve over the lamb burgers with a side salad of arugula.

Nutritions: *Calories 306 Fat 20g Carbs 10g Phosphorus 269mg Potassium (K) 492mg Sodium (Na) 86mg Protein 23g*

82. PORK LOINS WITH LEEKS

PREPARATION: 10 MIN   **COOKING: 35 MIN**   **SERVES: 2**

INGREDIENTS

- 1 sliced leek
- 1 tablespoon mustard seeds
- 6-ounce pork tenderloin
- 1 tablespoon cumin seeds
- 1 tablespoon dry mustard
- 1 tablespoon extra-virgin oil

DIRECTIONS

1. Preheat the broiler to medium high heat.
2. In a dry skillet heat mustard and cumin seeds until they start to pop (3-5 minutes).
3. Grind seeds using a pestle and mortar or blender and then mix in the dry mustard.
4. Coat the pork on both sides with the mustard blend and add to a baking tray to broil for 25-30 minutes or until cooked through. Turn once halfway through.
5. Remove and place to one side.
6. Heat the oil in a pan on medium heat and add the leeks for 5-6 minutes or until soft.
7. Serve the pork tenderloin on a bed of leeks and enjoy!

Nutritions: *Calories 139 Fat 5g Carbs 2g Phosphorus 278mg Potassium (K) 45mg Sodium (Na) 47mg Protein 18g*

83. CHINESE BEEF WRAPS

PREPARATION: 10 MIN   **COOKING: 30 MIN**   **SERVES: 2**

INGREDIENTS

- 2 iceberg lettuce leaves
- ½ diced cucumber
- 1 teaspoon canola oil
- 5-ounce lean ground beef
- 1 teaspoon ground ginger
- 1 tablespoon chili flakes
- 1 minced garlic clove
- 1 tablespoon rice wine vinegar

DIRECTIONS

1. Mix the ground meat with the garlic, rice wine vinegar, chili flakes and ginger in a bowl.
2. Heat oil in a skillet over medium heat.
3. Add the beef to the pan and cook for 20-25 minutes or until cooked through.
4. Serve beef mixture with diced cucumber in each lettuce wrap and fold.

Nutritions: *Calories 156 Fat 2g Carbs 4 G Phosphorus 1 Mg Sodium (Na) 54mg Protein 14g*

84. GRILLED SKIRT STEAK

PREPARATION: 15 MIN

COOKING: 8-9 MIN

SERVES: 4

INGREDIENTS

- 2 teaspoons fresh ginger herb, grated finely
- 2 teaspoons fresh lime zest, grated finely
- ¼ cup coconut sugar
- 2 teaspoons fish sauce
- 2 tablespoons fresh lime juice
- ½ cup coconut milk
- 1-pound beef skirt steak, trimmed and cut into 4-inch slices lengthwise
- Salt, to taste

DIRECTIONS

1. In a sizable sealable bag, mix together all ingredients except steak and salt.
2. Add steak and coat with marinade generously.
3. Seal the bag and refrigerate to marinate for about 4-12 hours.
4. Preheat the grill to high heat. Grease the grill grate.
5. Remove steak from refrigerator and discard the marinade.
6. With a paper towel, dry the steak and sprinkle with salt evenly.
7. Cook the steak for approximately 3½ minutes.
8. Flip the medial side and cook for around 2½-5 minutes or till desired doneness.
9. Remove from grill pan and keep side for approximately 5 minutes before slicing.
10. With a clear, crisp knife cut into desired slices and serve.

Nutritions: *Calories: 465 Fat: 10g Carbohydrates: 22g Fiber: 0g Protein: 37g Potassium (K) 492mg Sodium (Na)*

85. SPICY LAMB CURRY

PREPARATION: 15 MIN

COOKING: 2 H 15 MIN

SERVES: 6-8

INGREDIENTS

- 4 teaspoons ground coriander
- 4 teaspoons ground coriander
- 4 teaspoons ground cumin
- ¾ teaspoon ground ginger
- 2 teaspoons ground cinnamon
- ½ teaspoon ground cloves
- ½ teaspoon ground cardamom
- 2 tablespoons sweet paprika
- ½ tablespoon cayenne pepper
- 2 teaspoons chili powder
- 2 teaspoons salt
- 1 tablespoon coconut oil
- 2 pounds boneless lamb, trimmed and cubed into 1-inch size
- Salt and freshly ground black pepper, to taste
- 2 cups onions, chopped
- 1¼ cups water
- 1 cup coconut milk

DIRECTIONS

1. For spice mixture in a bowl, mix together all spices. Keep aside.
2. Season the lamb with salt and black pepper.
3. In a large dutch oven, heat oil on medium-high heat.
4. Add lamb and stir fry for around 5 minutes.
5. Add onion and cook approximately 4-5 minutes.
6. Stir in spice mixture and cook approximately 1 minute.
7. Add water and coconut milk and provide to some boil on high heat.
8. Reduce the heat to low and simmer, covered for approximately 1-120 minutes or till desired doneness of lamb.
9. Uncover and simmer for approximately 3-4 minutes.
10. Serve hot.

Nutritions: *Calories: 466 Fat: 10g Carbohydrates: 23g Fiber: 9g Protein: 36g Potassium (K) 492mg Sodium (Na)*

86. LAMB WITH PRUNES

PREPARATION: 15 MIN

COOKING: 2 H 40 MIN

SERVES: 4-6

INGREDIENTS

- 3 tablespoons coconut oil
- 2 onions, chopped finely
- 1 (1-inch) piece fresh ginger, minced
- 3 garlic cloves, minced
- ½ teaspoon ground turmeric
- 2 ½ pound lamb shoulder, trimmed and cubed into 3-inch size
- Salt and freshly ground black pepper, to taste
- ½ teaspoon saffron threads, crumbled
- 1 cinnamon stick
- 3 cups water
- 1 cup runes, pitted and halved

DIRECTIONS

1. In a big pan, melt coconut oil on medium heat.
2. Add onions, ginger, garlic cloves and turmeric and sauté for about 3-5 minutes.
3. Sprinkle the lamb with salt and black pepper evenly.
4. In the pan, add lamb and saffron threads and cook for approximately 4-5 minutes.
5. Add cinnamon stick and water and produce to some boil on high heat.
6. Reduce the temperature to low and simmer, covered for around 1½-120 minutes or till desired doneness of lamb.
7. Stir in prunes and simmer for approximately 20-a half-hour.
8. Remove cinnamon stick and serve hot.

Nutritions: *Calories: 393 Fat: 12g Carbohydrates: 10g Fiber: 4g Protein: 36g Potassium (K) 492mg Sodium (Na)*

87. ROAST BEEF

PREPARATION: 25 MIN

COOKING: 55 MIN

SERVES: 3

INGREDIENTS

- Quality rump or sirloin tip roast

DIRECTIONS

1. Place in roasting pan o n a shallow rack
2. Season with pepper and herbs
3. Insert meat thermometer in the center or thickest part of the roast
4. Roast to the desired degree of doneness
5. After removing from over for about 15 minutes let it chill
6. In the end the roast should be moister than well done.

Nutritions: *Calories 158 Protein 24 G Fat 6 G Carbs 0 G Phosphorus 206 Mg Potassium (K) 328 Mg Sodium (Na) 55 Mg*

88. BEEF BROCHETTES

PREPARATION: 20 MIN   **COOKING: 1 H**   **SERVES: 1**

INGREDIENTS

- 1 ½ cups pineapple chunks
- 1 sliced large onion
- 2 pounds thick steak
- 1 sliced medium bell pepper
- 1 bay leaf
- ¼ cup vegetable oil
- ½ cup lemon juice
- 2 crushed garlic cloves

DIRECTIONS

1. Cut beef cubes and place in a plastic bag
2. Combine marinade ingredients in small bowl
3. Mix and pour over beef cubes
4. Seal the bag and refrigerate for 3 to 5 hours
5. Divide ingredients onion, beef cube, green pepper, pineapple
6. Grill about 9 minutes each side

Nutritions: *Calories 304 Protein 35 G Fat 15 G Carbs 11 G Phosphorus 264 Mg Potassium (K) 388 Mg Sodium (Na) 70 Mg*

89. COUNTRY FRIED STEAK

PREPARATION: 10 MIN **COOKING: 1 H 40 MIN** **SERVES: 3**

INGREDIENTS

- 1 large onion
- ½ cup flour
- 3 tablespoons. Vegetable oil
- ¼ teaspoon pepper
- 1½ pounds round steak
- ½ teaspoon paprika

DIRECTIONS

1. Trim excess fat from steak
2. Cut into small pieces
3. Combine flour, paprika and pepper and mix together
4. Preheat skillet with oil
5. Cook steak on both sides
6. When the color of steak is brown remove to a platter
7. Add water (150 ml) and stir around the skillet
8. Return browned steak to skillet, if necessary, add water again so that bottom side of steak does not stick

Nutritions: *Calories 248 Protein 30 G Fat 10 G Carbs 5 G Phosphorus 190 Mg Potassium (K) 338 Mg Sodium (Na) 60 Mg*

90. BEEF POT ROAST

PREPARATION: 20 MIN

COOKING: 1 H

SERVES: 3

INGREDIENTS

- Round bone roast
- 2 - 4 pounds chuck roast

DIRECTIONS

1. Trim off excess fat
2. Place a tablespoon of oil in a large skillet and heat to medium
3. Roll pot roast in flour and brown on all sides in a hot skillet
4. After the meat gets a brown color, reduce heat to low
5. Season with pepper and herbs and add ½ cup of water
6. Cook slowly for 1½ hours or until it looks ready

Nutritions: *Calories 157 Protein 24g Fat 13g Carbs 0g Phosphorus 204Mg Sodium (Na) 50Mg*

91. HOMEMADE BURGERS

PREPARATION: 10 MIN   **COOKING: 20 MIN**   **SERVES: 2**

INGREDIENTS

- 4 ounce lean 100% ground beef
- 1 teaspoon black pepper
- 1 garlic clove, minced
- 1 teaspoon olive oil
- 1/4 cup onion, finely diced
- 1 tablespoon balsamic vinegar
- 1/2ounce brie cheese, crumbled
- 1 teaspoon mustard

DIRECTIONS

1. Season ground beef with pepper and then mix in minced garlic.
2. Form burger shapes with the ground beef using the palms of your hands.
3. Heat a skillet on a medium to high heat, and then add the oil.
4. Sauté the onions for 5-10 minutes until browned.
5. Then add the balsamic vinegar and sauté for another 5 minutes.
6. Remove and set aside.
7. Add the burgers to the pan and heat on the same heat for 5-6 minutes before flipping and heating for a further 5-6 minutes until cooked through.
8. Spread the mustard onto each burger.
9. Crumble the brie cheese over each burger and serve!
10. Try with a crunchy side salad!
11. Tip: if using fresh beef and not defrosted, prepare double the ingredients and freeze burgers in plastic wrap (after cooling) for up to 1 month.
12. Thoroughly defrost before heating through completely in the oven to serve.

Nutritions: *Calories: 178 Fat: 10g Carbohydrates: 4g Phosphorus: 147mg Potassium: 272mg Sodium: 273 Mg Protein: 16g*

92. SLOW-COOKED BEEF BRISKET

PREPARATION: 10 MIN

COOKING: 3 H 30 MIN

SERVES: 6

INGREDIENTS

- 10-ounce chuck roast
- 1 onion, sliced
- 1 cup carrots, peeled and sliced
- 1 tablespoon mustard
- 1 tablespoon thyme (fresh or dried)
- 1 tablespoon rosemary (fresh or dried)
- 2 garlic cloves
- 2 tablespoon extra-virgin olive oil
- 1 teaspoon black pepper
- 1 cup homemade chicken stock (p.52)
- 1 cup water

DIRECTIONS

1. Preheat oven to 300°f/150°c/gas mark 2.
2. Trim any fat from the beef and soak vegetables in warm water.
3. Make a paste by mixing together the mustard, thyme, rosemary, and garlic, before mixing in the oil and pepper.
4. Combine this mix with the stock.
5. Pour the mixture over the beef into an oven proof baking dish.
6. Place the vegetables onto the bottom of the baking dish with the beef.
7. Cover and roast for 3 hours, or until tender.
8. Uncover the dish and continue to cook for 30 minutes in the oven.
9. Serve hot!

Nutritions: *Calories: 151 Fat: 7g Carbohydrates: 7g Phosphorus: 144mg Potassium: 344mg Sodium: 279mg Protein: 15g*

CHAPTER 8. VEGETABLE MAINS RECIPES

93. RUTABAGA LATKES

PREPARATION: 15 MIN **COOKING: 7 MIN** **SERVES: 4**

INGREDIENTS

- 1 teaspoon hemp seeds
- 1 teaspoon ground black pepper
- 7 oz rutabaga, grated
- ½ teaspoon ground paprika
- 2 tablespoons coconut flour
- 1 egg, beaten
- 1 teaspoon olive oil

DIRECTIONS

1. Mix up together hemp seeds, ground black pepper, ground paprika, and coconut flour.
2. Then add grated rutabaga and beaten egg.
3. With the help of the fork combine together all the ingredients into the smooth mixture.
4. Preheat the skillet for 2-3 minutes over the high heat.
5. Then reduce the heat till medium and add olive oil.
6. With the help of the fork, place the small amount of rutabaga mixture in the skillet. Flatten it gently in the shape of latkes.
7. Cook the latkes for 3 minutes from each side.
8. After this, transfer them in the plate and repeat the same steps with remaining rutabaga mixture.

Nutritions: *Calories 64, Fat 3.1, Fiber 3, Carbs 7.1, Protein 2.8 Phosphorus: 110mg Potassium: 117mg Sodium: 75mg*

94. GLAZED SNAP PEAS

PREPARATION: 10 MIN　　　**COOKING: 5 MIN**　　　**SERVES: 2**

INGREDIENTS

- 1 cup snap peas
- 2 teaspoon Erythritol
- 1 teaspoon butter, melted
- ¾ teaspoon ground nutmeg
- ¼ teaspoon salt
- 1 cup water, for cooking

DIRECTIONS

1. Pour water in the pan. Add snap peas and bring them to boil.
2. Boil the snap peas for 5 minutes over the medium heat.
3. Then drain water and chill the snap peas.
4. Meanwhile, whisk together ground nutmeg, melted butter, salt, and Erythritol.
5. Preheat the mixture in the microwave oven for 5 seconds.
6. Pour the sweet butter liquid over the snap peas and shake them well.
7. The side dish should be served only warm.

Nutritions: *Calories 80 Fat 2.5 Fiber 3.9 Carbs 10.9 Protein 4 Phosphorus: 120mg Potassium: 137mg Sodium: 85mg*

95. STEAMED COLLARD GREENS

PREPARATION: 10 MIN

COOKING: 5 MIN

SERVES: 2

INGREDIENTS

- 2 cups Collard Greens
- 1 tablespoon lime juice
- 1 teaspoon olive oil
- 1 teaspoon sesame seeds
- ½ teaspoon chili flakes
- 1 cup water, for the steamer

DIRECTIONS

1. Chop collard greens roughly.
2. Pour water in the steamer and insert rack.
3. Place the steamer bowl, add collard greens, and close the lid.
4. Steam the greens for 5 minutes.
5. After this, transfer the steamed collard greens in the salad bowl.
6. Sprinkle it with the lime juice, olive oil, sesame seeds, and chili flakes.
7. Mix up greens with the help of 2 forks and leave to rest for 10 minutes before serving.

Nutritions: *Calories 43 Fat 3.4 Fiber 1.7 Carbs 3.4 Protein 1.3 Phosphorus: 130mg Potassium: 127mg Sodium: 85mg*

96. BAKED EGGPLANTS SLICES

PREPARATION: 15 MIN　　**COOKING: 15 MIN**　　**SERVES: 3**

INGREDIENTS

- 1 large eggplant, trimmed
- 1 tablespoon butter, softened
- 1 teaspoon minced garlic
- 1 teaspoon salt

DIRECTIONS

1. Slice the eggplant and sprinkle it with salt. Mix up well and leave for 10 minutes to make the vegetable "give" bitter juice.
2. After this, dry the eggplant with the paper towel.
3. In the shallow bowl, mix up together minced garlic and softened butter.
4. Brush every eggplant slice with the garlic mixture.
5. Line the baking tray with baking paper. Preheat the oven to 355F.
6. Place the sliced eggplants in the tray to make 1 layer and transfer it in the oven.
7. Bake the eggplants for 15 minutes. The cooked eggplants will be tender but not soft!

Nutritions: *Calories 81 Fat 4.2 Fiber 6.5 Carbs 11.1 Protein 1.9 Phosphorus: 110mg Potassium: 117mg Sodium: 75mg*

97. PESTO AVOCADO

PREPARATION: 10 MIN   **COOKING: 10 MIN**   **SERVES: 2**

INGREDIENTS

- 1 avocado, pitted, halved
- 1/3 cup Mozzarella balls, cherry size
- 1 cup fresh basil
- 1 tablespoon walnuts
- ¼ teaspoon garlic, minced
- ¾ teaspoon salt
- ¾ teaspoon ground black pepper
- 4 tablespoons olive oil
- 1 oz Parmesan, grated
- 1/3 cup cherry tomatoes

DIRECTIONS

1. Make pesto sauce: blend together salt, minced garlic, walnuts, fresh basil, ground black pepper, and olive oil.
2. When the mixture is smooth, add grated cheese and pulse it for 3 seconds more.
3. Then scoop ½ flesh from the avocado halves.
4. In the mixing bowl, mix up together mozzarella balls and cherry tomatoes.
5. Add pesto sauce and shake it well.
6. Preheat the oven to 360F.
7. Fill the avocado halves with the cherry tomato mixture and bake for 10 minutes.

Nutritions: *Calories 526 Fat 53.2 Fiber 7.8, Carbs 11.7 Protein 8.2 Phosphorus: 130mg Potassium: 147mg Sodium: 95mg*

98. VEGETABLE MASALA

PREPARATION: 10 MIN   **COOKING: 18 MIN**   **SERVES: 4**

INGREDIENTS

- 2 cups green beans, chopped
- 1 cup white mushroom, chopped
- ¾ cup tomatoes, crushed
- 1 teaspoon minced garlic
- 1 teaspoon minced ginger
- 1 teaspoon chili flakes
- 1 tablespoon garam masala
- 1 tablespoon olive oil
- 1 teaspoon salt

DIRECTIONS

1. Line the tray with parchment and preheat the oven to 360F.
2. Place the green beans and mushrooms in the tray.
3. Sprinkle the vegetables with crushed tomatoes, minced garlic and ginger, chili flakes, garam masala, olive oil, and salt.
4. Mix up well and transfer in the oven.
5. Cook vegetable masala for 18 minutes.

Nutritions: *Calories 60 Fat 30.7 Fiber 2.5 Carbs 6.4 Protein 2 Phosphorus: 110mg Potassium: 117mg Sodium: 75mg*

99. FAST CABBAGE CAKES

PREPARATION: 15 MIN

COOKING: 10 MIN

SERVES: 2

INGREDIENTS

- 1 cup cauliflower, shredded
- 1 egg, beaten
- 1 teaspoon salt
- 1 teaspoon ground black pepper
- 2 tablespoons almond flour
- 1 teaspoon olive oil

DIRECTIONS

1. Blend the shredded cabbage in the blender until you get cabbage rice.
2. Then mix up together cabbage rice with the egg, salt, ground black pepper, and almond flour.
3. Pour olive oil in the skillet and preheat it.
4. Then make the small cakes with the help of 2 spoons and place them in the hot oil.
5. Roast the cabbage cakes for 4 minutes from each side over the medium-low heat.
6. It is recommended to use a non-stick skillet.

Nutritions: *Calories 227 Fat 18.6 Fiber 4.5 Carbs 9.5 Protein 9.9 Phosphorus: 116mg Potassium: 137mg Sodium: 95mg*

100. CILANTRO CHILI BURGERS

PREPARATION: 10 MIN

COOKING: 15 MIN

SERVES: 3

INGREDIENTS

- 1 cup red cabbage
- 3 tablespoons almond flour
- 1 tablespoon cream cheese
- 1 oz scallions, chopped
- ½ teaspoon salt
- ½ teaspoon chili powder
- ½ cup fresh cilantro

DIRECTIONS

1. Chop red cabbage roughly and transfer in the blender.
2. Add fresh cilantro and blend the mixture until very smooth.
3. After this, transfer it in the bowl.
4. Add cream cheese, scallions, salt, chili powder, and almond flour.
5. Stir the mixture well.
6. Make 3 big burgers from the cabbage mixture or 6 small burgers.
7. Line the baking tray with baking paper.
8. Place the burgers in the tray.
9. Bake the cilantro burgers for 15 minutes at 360F.
10. Flip the burgers onto another side after 8 minutes of cooking.

Nutritions: *Calories 182 Fat 15.3 Fiber 4.1 Carbs 8.5 Protein 6.8 Phosphorus: 110mg Potassium: 117mg Sodium: 75mg*

101. JICAMA NOODLES

PREPARATION: 15 MIN

COOKING: 7 MIN

SERVES: 6

INGREDIENTS

- 1-pound jicama, peeled
- 2 tablespoons butter
- 1 teaspoon chili flakes
- 1 teaspoon salt
- ¾ cup of water

DIRECTIONS

1. Spiralize jicama with the help of spiralizer and place in jicama spirals in the saucepan.
2. Add butter, chili flakes, and salt.
3. Then add water and preheat the ingredients until the butter is melted.
4. Mix up it well.
5. Close the lid and cook noodles for 4 minutes over the medium heat.
6. Stir the jicama noodles well before transferring them in the serving plates.

Nutritions: *Calories 63 Fat 3.9 Fiber 3.7 Carbs 6.7 Protein 0.6 Phosphorus: 130mg Potassium: 127mg Sodium: 75mg*

102. CRACK SLAW

PREPARATION: 15 MIN

COOKING: 10 MIN

SERVES: 6

INGREDIENTS

- 1 cup cauliflower rice
- 1 tablespoon sriracha
- 1 teaspoon tahini paste
- 1 teaspoon sesame seeds
- 1 tablespoon lemon juice
- 1 teaspoon olive oil
- 1 teaspoon butter
- ½ teaspoon salt
- 2 cups coleslaw

DIRECTIONS

1. Toss the butter in the skillet and melt it.
2. Add cauliflower rice and sprinkle it with sriracha and tahini paste.
3. Mix up the vegetables and cook them for 10 minutes over the medium heat. Stir them from time to time.
4. When the cauliflower is cooked, transfer it into the big plate.
5. Add coleslaw and stir gently.
6. Then sprinkle the salad with sesame seeds, lemon juice, olive oil, and salt.
7. Mix up well.

Nutritions: *Calories 76 Fat 5.8 Fiber 0.6 Carbs 6 Protein 1.1 Phosphorus: 110mg Potassium: 117mg Sodium: 75mg*

103. CHOW MEIN

 PREPARATION: 10 MIN

 COOKING: 10 MIN

 SERVES: 6

INGREDIENTS

- 7 oz kelp noodles
- 5 oz broccoli florets
- 1 tablespoon tahini sauce
- ¼ teaspoon minced ginger
- 1 teaspoon Sriracha
- ½ teaspoon garlic powder
- 1 cup of water

DIRECTIONS

1. Pour water in the saucepan and bring it to boil.
2. Add broccoli and boil it for 4 minutes over the high heat.
3. Then drain water into the bowl and chill it tills the room temperature.
4. Soak the kelp noodles in the "broccoli water".
5. Meanwhile, place tahini sauce, sriracha, minced ginger, and garlic in the saucepan.
6. Bring the mixture to boil. Add oil if needed.
7. Then add broccoli and soaked noodles.
8. Add 3 tablespoons of "broccoli water".
9. Mix up the noodles and bring to boil.
10. Switch off the heat and transfer chow mein in the serving bowls.

Nutritions: *Calories 18 Fat 0.8 Fiber 0.7 Carbs 2.8 Protein 0.9 Phosphorus: 150mg Potassium: 127mg Sodium: 75mg*

104. MUSHROOM TACOS

PREPARATION: 10 MIN

COOKING: 15 MIN

SERVES: 6

INGREDIENTS

- 6 collard greens leaves
- 2 cups mushrooms, chopped
- 1 white onion, diced
- 1 tablespoon Taco seasoning
- 1 tablespoon coconut oil
- ½ teaspoon salt
- ¼ cup fresh parsley
- 1 tablespoon mayonnaise

DIRECTIONS

1. Put the coconut oil in the skillet and melt it.
2. Add chopped mushrooms and diced onion. Mix up the ingredients.
3. Close the lid and cook them for 10 minutes.
4. After this, sprinkle the vegetables with Taco seasoning, salt, and add fresh parsley.
5. Mix up the mixture and cook for 5 minutes more.
6. Then add mayonnaise and stir well.
7. Chill the mushroom mixture little.
8. Fill the collard green leaves with the mushroom mixture and fold up them.

Nutritions: *Calories 52 Fat 3.3 Fiber 1.2 Carbs 5.1 Protein 1.4 Phosphorus: 130mg Potassium: 127mg Sodium: 75mg*

105. LIME SPINACH AND CHICKPEAS SALAD

 PREPARATION: 10 MIN

 COOKING: 0 MIN

 SERVES: 4

INGREDIENTS

- 16 ounces canned chickpeas, drained and rinsed
- 2 cups baby spinach leaves
- ½ tablespoon lime juice
- 2 tablespoons olive oil
- 1 teaspoon cumin, ground
- A pinch of sea salt and black pepper
- ½ teaspoon chili flakes

DIRECTIONS

1. In a bowl, mix the chickpeas with the spinach and the rest of the ingredients, toss and serve cold.

Nutritions: *Calories 240 Fat 8.2 Fiber 5.3 Carbs 11.6 Protein 12 Phosphorus: 110mg Potassium: 117mg Sodium: 75mg*

106. MINTY OLIVES AND TOMATOES SALAD

PREPARATION: 10 MIN

COOKING: 0 MIN

SERVES: 4

INGREDIENTS

- 1 cup kalamata olives, pitted and sliced
- 1 cup black olives, pitted and halved
- 1 cup cherry tomatoes, halved
- 4 tomatoes, chopped
- 1 red onion, chopped
- 2 tablespoons oregano, chopped
- 1 tablespoon mint, chopped
- 2 tablespoons balsamic vinegar
- ¼ cup olive oil
- 2 teaspoons Italian herbs, dried
- A pinch of sea salt and black pepper

DIRECTIONS

1. In a salad bowl, mix the olives with the tomatoes and the rest of the ingredients, toss and serve cold.

Nutritions: *Calories 190 Fat 8.1 Fiber 5.8 Carbs 11.6 Protein 4.6 Phosphorus: 110mg Potassium: 117mg Sodium: 75mg*

107. BEANS AND CUCUMBER SALAD

PREPARATION: 10 MIN   **COOKING: 0 MIN**   **SERVES: 4**

INGREDIENTS

- 15 ounces canned great northern beans, drained and rinsed
- 2 tablespoons olive oil
- ½ cup baby arugula
- 1 cup cucumber, sliced
- 1 tablespoon parsley, chopped
- 2 tomatoes, cubed
- A pinch of sea salt and black pepper
- 2 tablespoon balsamic vinegar

DIRECTIONS

1. In a bowl, mix the beans with the cucumber and the rest of the ingredients, toss and serve cold.

Nutritions: *Calories 233 Fat 9 Fiber 6.5 Carbs 13 Protein 8 Phosphorus: 210mg Potassium: 127mg Sodium: 85mg*

108. BROCCOLI PANCAKE

PREPARATION: 10 MIN

COOKING: 5 MIN

SERVES: 4

INGREDIENTS

- 3 cups broccoli florets, diced
- 2 eggs, beaten
- 2 tablespoons all-purpose flour
- 1/2 cup onion, chopped
- 2 tablespoons olive oil

DIRECTIONS

1. Boil broccoli in water for 5 minutes. Drain and set aside.
2. Mix egg and flour.
3. Add onion and broccoli to the mixture.
4. Cook the broccoli pancake until brown on both sides.

Nutritions: *Calories 140 Protein 6g Carbohydrates 7g Fat 10g Cholesterol 106mg Sodium 58mg Potassium 276mg Phosphorus 101mg Calcium 50mg Fiber 2.1g*

109. CARROT CASSEROLE

PREPARATION: 10 MIN   **COOKING: 20 MIN**   **SERVES: 8**

INGREDIENTS

- 1-pound carrots, sliced into rounds
- 12 low-sodium crackers
- 2 tablespoons butter
- 2 tablespoons onion, chopped
- 1/4 cup cheddar cheese, shredded

DIRECTIONS

1. Preheat your oven to 35o degrees f.
2. Boil carrots in a pot of water until tender.
3. Drain the carrots and reserve ¼ cup liquid.
4. Mash carrots.
5. Add all the ingredients into the carrots except cheese.
6. Place the mashed carrots in a casserole dish.
7. Sprinkle cheese on top and bake in the oven for 15 minutes.

Nutritions: *Calories 97 Protein 2g Carbohydrates 9g Fat 7g Cholesterol 13mg Sodium 174mg Potassium 153mg Phosphorus 47mg Calcium 66mg Fiber 1.8g*

110. CAULIFLOWER RICE

PREPARATION: 10 MIN

COOKING: 10 MIN

SERVES: 4

INGREDIENTS

- 1 head cauliflower, sliced into florets
- 1 tablespoon butter
- Black pepper to taste
- 1/4 teaspoon garlic powder
- 1/4 teaspoon herb seasoning blend

DIRECTIONS

1. Put cauliflower florets in a food processor.
2. Pulse until consistency is similar to grain.
3. In a pan over medium heat, melt the butter and add the spices.
4. Toss cauliflower rice and cook for 10 minutes.
5. Fluff using a fork before serving.

Nutritions: *Calories 47 Protein 1g Carbohydrates 4g Fat 3g Cholesterol 8mg Sodium 43mg Potassium 206mg Phosphorus 31mg Calcium 16mg Fiber 1.4g*

111. EGGPLANT FRIES

PREPARATION: 10 MIN

COOKING: 5 MIN

SERVES: 6

INGREDIENTS

- 2 eggs, beaten
- 1 cup almond milk
- 1 teaspoon hot sauce
- 3/4 cup cornstarch
- 3 teaspoons dry ranch seasoning mix
- 3/4 cup dry bread crumbs
- 1 eggplant, sliced into strips
- 1/2 cup oil

DIRECTIONS

1. In a bowl, mix eggs, milk and hot sauce.
2. In a dish, mix cornstarch, seasoning and breadcrumbs.
3. Dip first the eggplant strips in the egg mixture.
4. Coat each strip with the cornstarch mixture.
5. Pour oil in a pan over medium heat.
6. Once hot, add the fries and cook for 3 minutes or until golden.

Nutritions: *Calories 234 Protein 7g Carbohydrates 25g Fat 13g Cholesterol 48mg Sodium 212mg Potassium 215mg Phosphorus 86mg Calcium 70mg Fiber 2.1g*

112. SEASONED GREEN BEANS

PREPARATION: 10 MIN   **COOKING: 10 MIN**   **SERVES: 4**

INGREDIENTS

- 10-ounce green beans
- 4 teaspoons butter
- 1/4 cup onion, chopped
- 1/2 cup red bell pepper, chopped
- 1 teaspoon dried dill weed
- 1 teaspoon dried parsley
- 1/4 teaspoon black pepper

DIRECTIONS

1. Boil green beans in a pot of water. Drain.
2. In a pan over medium heat, melt the butter and cook onion and bell pepper.
3. Season with dill and parsley.
4. Put the green beans back to the skillet.
5. Sprinkle pepper on top before serving.

Nutritions: *Calories 67 Protein 2g Carbohydrates 8g Fat 3g Cholesterol 0mg Sodium 55mg Potassium 194mg Phosphorus 32mg Calcium 68mg Fiber 4.0g*

113. GRILLED SQUASH

 PREPARATION: 10 MIN

 COOKING: 6 MIN

 SERVES: 8

INGREDIENTS

- 4 zucchinis, rinsed, drained and sliced
- 4 crookneck squash, rinsed, drained and sliced
- Cooking spray
- 1/4 teaspoon garlic powder
- 1/4 teaspoon black pepper

DIRECTIONS

1. Arrange squash on a baking sheet.
2. Spray with oil.
3. Season with garlic powder and pepper.
4. Grill for 3 minutes per side or until tender but not too soft.

Nutritions: *Calories 17 Protein 1g Carbohydrates 3g Fat 0g Cholesterol 0mg Sodium 6mg Potassium 262mg Phosphorus 39mg Calcium 16mg Fiber 1.1g*

114. THAI TOFU BROTH

PREPARATION: 5 MIN

COOKING: 15 MIN

SERVES: 4

INGREDIENTS

- 1 cup rice noodles
- ½ sliced onion
- 6 ounce drained, pressed and cubed tofu
- ¼ cup sliced scallions
- ½ cup water
- ½ cup canned water chestnuts
- ½ cup rice milk
- 1 tablespoon lime juice
- 1 tablespoon coconut oil
- ½ finely sliced chili
- 1 cup snow peas

DIRECTIONS

1. Heat the oil in a wok on a high heat and then sauté the tofu until brown on each side.
2. Add the onion and sauté for 2-3 minutes.
3. Add the rice milk and water to the wok until bubbling.
4. Lower to medium heat and add the noodles, chili and water chestnuts.
5. Allow to simmer for 10-15 minutes and then add the sugar snap peas for 5 minutes.
6. Serve with a sprinkle of scallions.

Nutritions: *Calories 304 Protein 9g Carbs 38g Fat 13g Sodium (Na) 36mg Potassium (K) 114mg Phosphorus 101mg*

115. DELICIOUS VEGETARIAN LASAGNA

PREPARATION: 10 MIN

COOKING: 1 H

SERVES: 4

INGREDIENTS

- 1 teaspoon basil
- 1 tablespoon olive oil
- ½ sliced red pepper
- 3 lasagna sheets
- ½ diced red onion
- ¼ teaspoon black pepper
- 1 cup rice milk
- 1 minced garlic clove
- 1 cup sliced eggplant
- ½ sliced zucchini
- ½ pack soft tofu
- 1 teaspoon oregano

DIRECTIONS

1. Preheat oven to 325°f/gas mark 3.
2. Slice zucchini, eggplant and pepper into vertical strips.
3. Add the rice milk and tofu to a food processor and blitz until smooth. Set aside.
4. Heat the oil in a skillet over medium heat and add the onions and garlic for 3-4 minutes or until soft.
5. Sprinkle in the herbs and pepper and allow to stir through for 5-6 minutes until hot.
6. Into a lasagna or suitable oven dish, layer 1 lasagna sheet, then 1/3 the eggplant, followed by 1/3 zucchini, then 1/3 pepper before pouring over 1/3 of tofu white sauce.
7. Repeat for the next 2 layers, finishing with the white sauce.
8. Add to the oven for 40-50 minutes or until veg is soft and can easily be sliced into servings.

Nutritions: *Calories 235 Protein 5g Carbs 10g Fat 9g Sodium (Na) 35mg Potassium (K) 129mg Phosphorus 66mg*

116. CHILI TOFU NOODLES

PREPARATION: 5 MIN COOKING: 15 MIN SERVES: 4

INGREDIENTS

- ½ diced red chili
- 2 cups rice noodles
- ½ juiced lime
- 6 ounce pressed and cubed silken firm tofu
- 1 teaspoon grated fresh ginger
- 1 tablespoon coconut oil
- 1 cup green beans
- 1 minced garlic clove

DIRECTIONS

1. Steam the green beans for 10-12 minutes or according to package directions and drain.
2. Cook the noodles in a pot of boiling water for 10-15 minutes or according to package directions.
3. Meanwhile, heat a wok or skillet on a high heat and add coconut oil.
4. Now add the tofu, chili flakes, garlic and ginger and sauté for 5-10 minutes.
5. After doing that, drain in the noodles along with the green beans and lime juice then add it to the wok.
6. Toss to coat.
7. Serve hot!

Nutritions: *Calories 246 Protein 10g Carbs 28g Fat 12g Sodium (Na) 25mg Potassium (K) 126mg Phosphorus 79mg*

117. CURRIED CAULIFLOWER

PREPARATION: 5 MIN

COOKING: 20 MIN

SERVES: 4

INGREDIENTS

- 1 teaspoon turmeric
- 1 diced onion
- 1 tablespoon chopped fresh cilantro
- 1 teaspoon cumin
- ½ diced chili
- ½ cup water
- 1 minced garlic clove
- 1 tablespoon coconut oil
- 1 teaspoon garam masala
- 2 cups cauliflower florets

DIRECTIONS

1. Add the oil to a skillet on medium heat.
2. Sauté the onion and garlic for 5 minutes until soft.
3. Add in the cumin, turmeric and garam masala and stir to release the aromas.
4. Now add the chili to the pan along with the cauliflower.
5. Stir to coat.
6. Pour in the water and reduce the heat to a simmer for 15 minutes.
7. Garnish with cilantro to serve.

Nutritions: *Calories 108 Protein 2 G Carbs 11g Fat 7g Sodium (Na) 35mg Potassium (K) 328 Mg Phosphorus 39mg*

118. ELEGANT VEGGIE TORTILLAS

PREPARATION: 30 MIN

COOKING: 15 MIN

SERVES: 12

INGREDIENTS

- 1½ cups of chopped broccoli florets
- 1½ cups of chopped cauliflower florets
- 1 tablespoon of water
- 2 teaspoon of canola oil
- 1½ cups of chopped onion
- 1 minced garlic clove
- 2 tablespoons of finely chopped fresh parsley
- 1 cup of low-cholesterol liquid egg substitute
- Freshly ground black pepper, to taste
- 4 (6-ounce) warmed corn tortillas

DIRECTIONS

1. In a microwave bowl, place broccoli, cauliflower and water and microwave, covered for about 3-5 minutes.
2. Remove from microwave and drain any liquid.
3. Heat oil on medium heat.
4. Add onion and sauté for about 4-5 minutes.
5. Add garlic and then sauté it for about 1 minute.
6. Stir in broccoli, cauliflower, parsley, egg substitute and black pepper.
7. Reduce the heat and it to simmer for about 10 minutes.
8. Remove from heat and keep aside to cool slightly.
9. Place broccoli mixture over ¼ of each tortilla.
10. Fold the outside edges inward and roll up like a burrito.
11. Secure each tortilla with toothpicks to secure the filling.
12. Cut each tortilla in half and serve.

Nutritions: *Calories: 217 Fat: 3.3g Carbs: 41g Protein: 8.1g Fiber: 6.3g Potassium: 289mg Sodium: 87mg*

119. SIMPLE BROCCOLI STIR-FRY

PREPARATION: 40 MIN

COOKING: 15 MIN

SERVES: 4

INGREDIENTS

- 1 tablespoon of olive oil
- 1 minced garlic clove
- 2 cups of broccoli florets
- 2 tablespoons of water

DIRECTIONS

1. Heat oil on medium heat.
2. Add garlic and then sauté for about 1 minute.
3. Add the broccoli and stir fry for about 2 minutes.
4. Stir in water and stir fry for about 4-5 minutes.
5. Serve warm.

Nutritions: *Calories: 47 Fat: 3.6g Carbs: 3.3g Protein: 1.3g Fiber: 1.2g Potassium: 147mg Sodium: 15mg*

120. SALAD WITH STRAWBERRIES AND GOAT CHEESE

PREPARATION: 15 MIN

COOKING: 0 MIN

SERVES: 2

INGREDIENTS

- Baby lettuce, to taste
- 1-pint strawberries
- Balsamic vinegar
- Extra virgin olive oil
- 1/4 teaspoon black pepper
- 8-ounce soft goat cheese

DIRECTIONS

1. Prepare the lettuce by washing and drying it, then cut the strawberries.
2. Cut the soft goat cheese into 8 pieces.
3. Put together the balsamic vinegar and the extra virgin olive oil in a large cup with a whisk.
4. Mix the strawberries pressing them and putting them in a bowl, add the dressing and mix, then divide the lettuce into four dishes and cut the other strawberries, arranging them on the salad.
5. Put cheese slices on top and add pepper. Serve and enjoy!

Nutritions: *Calories: 300 Protein: 13g Sodium: 285mg Potassium: 400mg Phosphorus: 193mg*

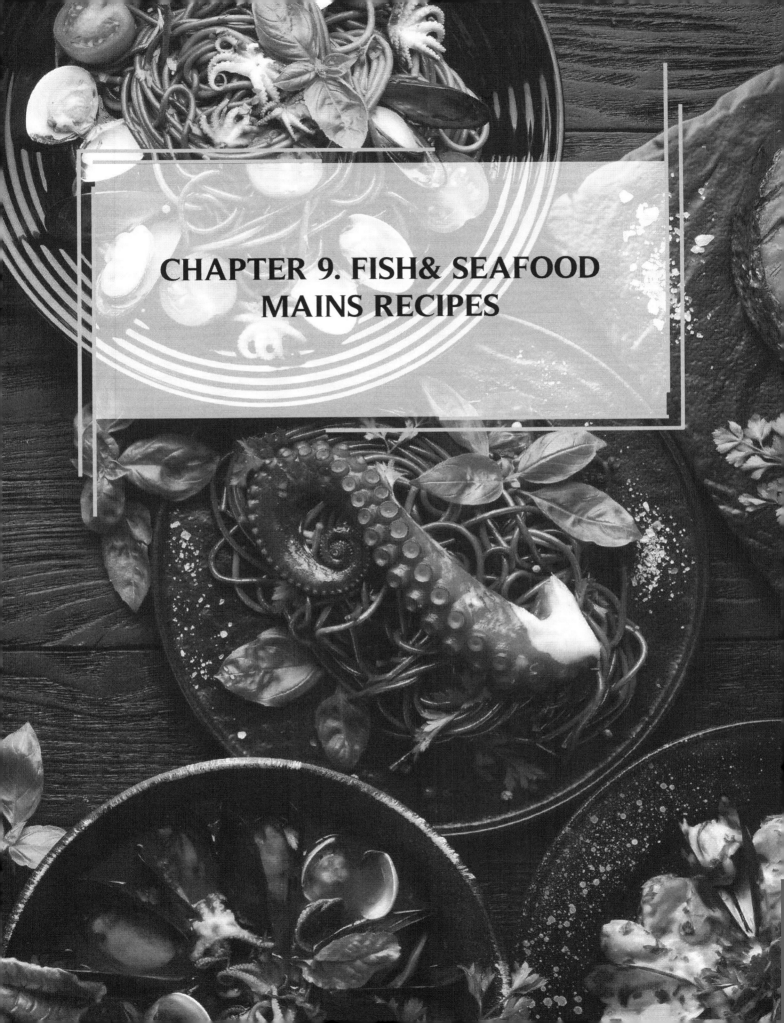

CHAPTER 9. FISH& SEAFOOD MAINS RECIPES

121. CURRIED FISH CAKES

PREPARATION: 10 MIN

COOKING: 18 MIN

SERVES: 4

INGREDIENTS

- ¾ pound Atlantic cod, cubed
- 1 apple, peeled and cubed
- 1 tablespoon yellow curry paste
- 2 tablespoons cornstarch
- 1 tablespoon peeled grated ginger root
- 1 large egg
- 1 tablespoon freshly squeezed lemon juice
- ⅛ teaspoon freshly ground black pepper
- ½ cup crushed puffed rice cereal
- 1 tablespoon olive oil

DIRECTIONS

1. Put the cod, apple, curry, cornstarch, ginger, egg, lemon juice, and pepper in a blender or food processor and process until finely chopped. Avoid over-processing, or the mixture will become mushy.
2. Place the rice cereal on a shallow plate.
3. Form the mixture into 8 patties.
4. Dredge the patties in the rice cereal to coat.
5. Cook patties for 3 to 5 minutes per side, turning once until a meat thermometer registers 160°f.
6. Serve.

Nutritions: *Calories: 188 Total Fat: 6g Saturated Fat: 1g Sodium: 150mg Potassium: 292mg Phosphorus: 150mg Carbohydrates: 12g Fiber: 1g Protein: 21g Sugar: 5g*

122. BAKED SOLE WITH CARAMELIZED ONION

PREPARATION: 10 MIN

COOKING: 20 MIN

SERVES: 4

INGREDIENTS

- 1 cup finely chopped onion
- ½ cup low-sodium vegetable broth
- 1 yellow summer squash, sliced
- 2 cups frozen broccoli florets
- 4 (3-ounce) fillets of sole
- Pinch salt
- 2 tablespoons olive oil
- Pinch baking soda
- 2 teaspoons avocado oil
- 1 teaspoon dried basil leaves

DIRECTIONS

1. Preheat the oven to 425°f.
2. Add the onions. Cook for 1 minute; then, stirring constantly, cook for another 4 minutes.
3. Remove the onions from the heat.
4. Pour the broth into a baking sheet with a lip and arrange the squash and broccoli on the sheet in a single layer. Top the vegetables with the fish. Sprinkle the fish with the salt and drizzle everything with the olive oil.
5. Bake the fish and the vegetables for 10 minutes.
6. While the fish is baking, return the skillet with the onions to medium-high heat and stir in a pinch of baking soda. Stir in the avocado oil and cook for 5 minutes, stirring frequently, until the onions are dark brown.
7. Transfer the onions to a plate.
8. Top the fish evenly with the onions. Sprinkle with the basil.
9. Return the fish to the oven, after this bake it 8 to10 minutes serve the fish on the vegetables.

Nutritions: *Calories: 202 Total Fat: 11g Saturated Fat: 3g Sodium: 320mg Potassium: 537 Phosphorus: 331mg Carbohydrates: 10g Fiber: 3g Protein: 16g Sugar: 4g*

123. THAI TUNA WRAPS

PREPARATION: 10 MIN   **COOKING: 0 MIN**   **SERVES: 4**

INGREDIENTS

- ¼ cup unsalted peanut butter
- 2 tablespoons freshly squeezed lemon juice
- 1 teaspoon low-sodium soy sauce
- ½ teaspoon ground ginger
- ⅛ teaspoon cayenne pepper
- 1 (6-ounce) can no-salt-added or low-sodium chunk light tuna, drained
- 1 cup shredded red cabbage
- 2 scallions, white and green parts, chopped
- 1 cup grated carrots
- 8 butter lettuce leaves

DIRECTIONS

1. In a medium bowl, stir together the peanut butter, lemon juice, soy sauce, ginger, and cayenne pepper until well combined.
2. Stir in the tuna, cabbage, scallions, and carrots.
3. Divide the tuna filling evenly between the butter lettuce leaves and serve.

Nutritions: *Calories: 175 Total Fat; 10g Saturated Fat: 1g Sodium: 98mg Potassium: 421mg Phosphorus: 153mg Carbohydrates: 8g Fiber: 2g Protein: 17g Sugar: 4g*

124. GRILLED FISH AND VEGETABLE PACKETS

PREPARATION: 15 MIN

COOKING: 12 MIN

SERVES: 4

INGREDIENTS

- 1 (8-ounce) package sliced mushrooms
- 1 leek, white and green parts, chopped
- 1 cup frozen corn
- 4 (4-ounce) atlantic cod fillets
- Juice of 1 lemon
- 3 tablespoons olive oil

DIRECTIONS

1. Prepare and preheat the grill to medium coals and set a grill 6 inches from the coals.
2. Tear off four 30-inch long strips of heavy-duty aluminum foil.
3. Arrange the mushrooms, leek, and corn in the center of each piece of foil and top with the fish.
4. Drizzle the packet contents evenly with the lemon juice and olive oil.
5. Bring the longer length sides of the foil together at the top and, holding the edges together, fold them over twice and then fold in the width sides to form a sealed packet with room for the steam.
6. Put the packets on the grill and grill for 10 to 12 minutes until the vegetables are tender-crisp and the fish flakes when tested with a fork. Be careful opening the packets because the escaping steam can be scalding.

Nutritions: *Calories: 267 Total Fat: 12g Saturated Fat: 2g Sodium: 97mg Potassium: 582mg Phosphorus: 238mg Carbohydrates: 13g Fiber: 2g Protein: 29g Sugar: 3g*

125. WHITE FISH SOUP

PREPARATION: 15 MIN

COOKING: 20 MIN

SERVES: 4

INGREDIENTS

- 2 tablespoons olive oil
- 1 onion, finely diced
- 1 green bell pepper, chopped
- 1 rib celery, thinly sliced
- 3 cups chicken broth, or more to taste
- 1/4 cup chopped fresh parsley
- 1 1/2 pounds cod, cut into 3/4-inch cubes
- Pepper to taste
- 1 dash red pepper flakes

DIRECTIONS

1. Heat oil in a soup pot over medium heat.
2. Add onion, bell pepper, and celery and cook until wilted, about 5 minutes.
3. Add broth and then bring to a simmer, about 5 minutes.
4. Cook 15 to 20 minutes.
5. Add cod, parsley, and red pepper flakes and simmer until fish flakes easily with a fork, 8 to 10 minutes more.
6. Season with black pepper.

Nutritions: *Calories 117 Total Fat 7.2g Saturated Fat 1.4g Cholesterol 18mg Sodium 37mg Total Carbohydrate 5.4g Dietary Fiber 1.3g Total Sugars 2.8g Protein 8.1g Calcium 23mg Iron 1mg Potassium 122mg Phosphorus 111 Mg*

126. LEMON BUTTER SALMON

PREPARATION: 15 MIN

COOKING: 15 MIN

SERVES: 6

INGREDIENTS

- 1 tablespoon butter
- 2 tablespoons olive oil
- 1 tablespoon dijon mustard
- 1 tablespoons lemon juice
- 2 cloves garlic, crushed
- 1 teaspoon dried dill
- 1 teaspoon dried basil leaves
- 1 tablespoon capers
- 24-ounce salmon filet

DIRECTIONS

1. Put all of the ingredients except the salmon in a saucepan over medium heat.
2. Bring to a boil and then simmer for 5 minutes.
3. Preheat your grill.
4. Create a packet using foil.
5. Place the sauce and salmon inside.
6. Seal the packet.
7. Grill for 12 minutes.

Nutritions: *Calories 292 Protein 22g Carbohydrates 2g Fat 22g Cholesterol 68mg Sodium 190mg Potassium 439mg Phosphorus 280mg Calcium 21mg*

127. CRAB CAKE

PREPARATION: 15 MIN

COOKING: 9 MIN

SERVES: 6

INGREDIENTS

- 1/4 cup onion, chopped
- 1/4 cup bell pepper, chopped
- 1 egg, beaten
- 6 low-sodium crackers, crushed
- 1/4 cup low-fat mayonnaise
- 1-pound crab meat
- 1 tablespoon dry mustard
- Pepper to taste
- 2 tablespoons lemon juice
- 1 tablespoon fresh parsley
- 1 tablespoon garlic powder
- 3 tablespoons olive oil

DIRECTIONS

1. Mix all the ingredients except the oil.
2. Form 6 patties from the mixture.
3. Pour the oil into a pan in a medium heat.
4. Cook the crab cakes for 5 minutes.
5. Flip and cook for another 4 minutes.

Nutritions: *Calories 189 Protein 13g Carbohydrates 5g Fat 14g Cholesterol 111mg Sodium 342mg Potassium 317mg Phosphorus 185mg Calcium 52mg Fiber 0.5g*

128. BAKED FISH IN CREAM SAUCE

PREPARATION: 10 MIN

COOKING: 40 MIN

SERVES: 4

INGREDIENTS

- 1-pound haddock
- 1/2 cup all-purpose flour
- 2 tablespoons butter (unsalted)
- 1/4 teaspoon pepper
- 2 cups fat-free nondairy creamer
- 1/4 cup water

DIRECTIONS

1. Preheat your oven to 350 degrees f.
2. Spray baking pan with oil.
3. Sprinkle with a little flour.
4. Arrange fish on the pan
5. Season with pepper.
6. Sprinkle remaining flour on the fish.
7. Spread creamer on both sides of the fish.
8. Bake for 40 minutes or until golden.
9. Spread cream sauce on top of the fish before serving.

Nutritions: *Calories 383 Protein 24g Carbohydrates 46g Fat 11g Cholesterol 79mg Sodium 253mg Potassium 400mg Phosphorus 266mg Calcium 46mg Fiber 0.4g*

129. SHRIMP & BROCCOLI

PREPARATION: 10 MIN

COOKING: 5 MIN

SERVES: 4

INGREDIENTS

- 1 tablespoon olive oil
- 1 clove garlic, minced
- 1-pound shrimp
- 1/4 cup red bell pepper
- 1 cup broccoli florets, steamed
- 10-ounce cream cheese
- 1/2 teaspoon garlic powder
- 1/4 cup lemon juice
- 3/4 teaspoon ground peppercorns
- 1/4 cup half and half creamer

DIRECTIONS

1. Pour the oil and cook garlic for 30 seconds.
2. Add shrimp and cook for 2 minutes.
3. Add the rest of the ingredients.
4. Mix well.
5. Cook for 2 minutes.

Nutritions: *Calories 469 Protein 28g Carbohydrates 28g Fat 28g Cholesterol 213mg Sodium 374mg Potassium 469mg Phosphorus 335mg Calcium 157mg Fiber 2.6g*

130. SHRIMP IN GARLIC SAUCE

PREPARATION: 10 MIN

COOKING: 6 MIN

SERVES: 4

INGREDIENTS

- 3 tablespoons butter (unsalted)
- 1/4 cup onion, minced
- 3 cloves garlic, minced
- 1-pound shrimp, shelled and deveined
- 1/2 cup half and half creamer
- 1/4 cup white wine
- 2 tablespoons fresh basil
- Black pepper to taste

DIRECTIONS

1. Add butter to a pan over medium low heat.
2. Let it melt.
3. Add the onion and garlic.
4. Cook for it 1-2 minutes.
5. Add the shrimp and cook for 2 minutes.
6. Transfer shrimp on a serving platter and set aside.
7. Add the rest of the ingredients.
8. Simmer for 3 minutes.
9. Pour sauce over the shrimp and serve.

Nutritions: *Calories 482 Protein 33g Carbohydrates 46g Fat 11g Cholesterol 230mg Sodium 213mg Potassium 514mg Phosphorus 398mg Calcium 133mg Fiber 2.0g*

131. FISH TACO

PREPARATION: 40 MIN **COOKING: 10 MIN** **SERVES: 6**

INGREDIENTS

- 1 tablespoon lime juice
- 1 tablespoon olive oil
- 1 clove garlic, minced
- 1-pound cod fillets
- 1/2 teaspoon ground cumin
- 1/4 teaspoon black pepper
- 1/2 teaspoon chili powder
- 1/4 cup sour cream
- 1/2 cup mayonnaise
- 2 tablespoons nondairy milk
- 1 cup cabbage, shredded
- 1/2 cup onion, chopped
- 1/2 bunch cilantro, chopped
- 12 corn tortillas

DIRECTIONS

1. Drizzle lemon juice over the fish fillet.
2. And then coat it with olive oil and then season with garlic, cumin, pepper and chili powder.
3. Let it sit for 30 minutes.
4. Broil fish for 10 minutes, flipping halfway through.
5. Flake the fish using a fork.
6. In a bowl, mix sour cream, milk and mayo.
7. Assemble tacos by filling each tortilla with mayo mixture, cabbage, onion, cilantro and fish flakes.

Nutritions: *Calories 366 Protein 18g Carbohydrates 31g Fat 19g Cholesterol 40mg Sodium 194mg Potassium 507mg Phosphorus 327mg Calcium 138mg Fiber 4.3g*

132. BAKED TROUT

PREPARATION: 5 MIN   **COOKING: 10 MIN**   **SERVES: 8**

INGREDIENTS

- 2-pound trout fillet
- 1 tablespoon oil
- 1 teaspoon salt-free lemon pepper
- 1/2 teaspoon paprika

DIRECTIONS

1. Preheat your oven to 350 degrees f.
2. Coat fillet with oil.
3. Place fish on a baking pan.
4. Season with lemon pepper and paprika.
5. Bake for 10 minutes.

Nutritions: *Calories 161 Protein 21g Carbohydrates 0g Fat 8g Cholesterol 58mg Sodium 109mg Potassium 38mg Phosphorus 227mg Calcium 75mg Fiber 0.1g*

133. FISH WITH MUSHROOMS

PREPARATION: 5 MIN

COOKING: 16 MIN

SERVES: 4

INGREDIENTS

- 1-pound cod fillet
- 2 tablespoons butter
- ¼ cup white onion, chopped
- 1 cup fresh mushrooms
- 1 teaspoon dried thyme

DIRECTIONS

1. Put the fish in a baking pan.
2. Preheat your oven to 450 degrees f.
3. Melt the butter and cook onion and mushroom for 1 minute.
4. Spread mushroom mixture on top of the fish.
5. Season with thyme.
6. Bake in the oven for 15 minutes.

Nutritions: *Calories 156 Protein 21g Carbohydrates 3g Fat 7g Cholesterol 49mg Sodium 110mg Potassium 561mg Phosphorus 225mg Calcium 30mg Fiber 0.5g*

134. EASY SALMON AND BRUSSELS SPROUTS

PREPARATION: 10 MIN

COOKING: 10 MIN

SERVES: 6

INGREDIENTS

- 6 deboned medium salmon fillets
- 1 tsp. onion powder
- 1 ¼ lbs. halved Brussels sprouts
- 3 tbsps. Extra virgin extra virgin olive oil
- 2 tbsps. Brown sugar
- 1 tsp. garlic powder
- 1 tsp. smoked paprika

DIRECTIONS

1. In a bowl, mix sugar with onion powder, garlic powder, smoked paprika as well as a number of tablespoon olive oil and whisk well.
2. Spread Brussels sprouts about the lined baking sheet, drizzle the rest in the essential extra virgin olive oil, toss to coat, introduce in the oven at 450 0F and bake for 5 minutes.
3. Add salmon fillets brush with sugar mix you've prepared, introduce inside the oven and bake for 15 minutes more.
4. Divide everything between plates and serve.
5. Enjoy!

Nutritions: *Calories: 212 Fat:5 g Carbs:12 g Protein:8 g Sugars:3.7 g Sodium:299.1 mg*

135. SALMON IN DILL SAUCE

PREPARATION: 10 MIN

COOKING: 10 MIN

SERVES: 6

INGREDIENTS

- 6 salmon fillets
- 1 c. low-fat, low-sodium chicken broth
- 1 tsp. cayenne pepper
- 2 tbsps. Fresh lemon juice
- 2 c. water
- ¼ c. chopped fresh dill

DIRECTIONS

1. In a slow cooker, mix together water, broth, lemon juice, lemon juice and dill.
2. Arrange salmon fillets on top, skin side down.
3. Sprinkle with cayenne pepper.
4. Set the slow cooker on low.
5. Cover and cook for about 1-2 hours.

Nutritions: *Calories: 360 Fat:8 g Carbs:44 g Protein:28 g Sugars:0.5 g Sodium:8 mg*

136. SHRIMP LO MEIN

PREPARATION: 10 MIN

COOKING: 10 MIN

SERVES: 6

INGREDIENTS

- 1 tbsp. cornstarch
- 1 lb. medium-size frozen raw shrimp
- 1 c. frozen shelled edamame
- 3 tbsps. Light teriyaki sauce
- 16 0z. Drained and rinsed tofu spaghetti noodles
- 18 oz. frozen Szechuan vegetable blend with sesame sauce

DIRECTIONS

1. Microwave noodles for 1 minute; set aside. Place shrimp in a small bowl and toss with 2 tablespoons teriyaki sauce; set aside.
2. Place mixed vegetables and edamame in a large nonstick skillet with 1/4 cup water. Cover and cook, stirring occasionally, over medium-high heat for 7 minutes or until cooked through.
3. Stir shrimp into vegetable mixture; cover and cook 4 to 5 minutes or until shrimp is pink and cooked through.
4. Stir together remaining 1 tablespoon teriyaki sauce and the cornstarch, then stir into the mixture in the skillet until thickened. Gently stir noodles into skillet and cook until warmed through.

Nutritions: *Calories: 252 Fat:7.1 g Carbs:35.2 g Protein:12.1 g Sugars:2.2 g Sodium:180 mg*

137. SALMON AND POTATOES MIX

PREPARATION: 10 MIN　　**COOKING: 10 MIN**　　**SERVES: 4**

INGREDIENTS

- 4 oz. chopped smoked salmon
- 1 tbsp. essential olive oil
- Black pepper
- 1 tbsp. chopped chives
- ¼ c. coconut cream
- 1 ½ lbs. chopped potatoes
- 2 tsps. Prepared horseradish

DIRECTIONS

1. Heat up a pan using the oil over medium heat, add potatoes and cook for 10 minutes.
2. Add salmon, chives, horseradish, cream and black pepper, toss, cook for 1 minute more, divide between plates and serve.
3. Enjoy!

Nutritions: *Calories: 233 Fat:6 g Carbs:9 g Protein:11 g Sugars:3.3 g Sodium:97 mg*

138. SMOKED SALMON AND RADISHES

PREPARATION: 10 MIN

COOKING: 10 MIN

SERVES: 8

INGREDIENTS

- ½ c. drained and chopped capers
- 1 lb. skinless, de-boned and flaked smoked salmon
- 4 chopped radishes
- 3 tbsps. Chopped chives
- 3 tbsps. Prepared beet horseradish
- 2 tsps. Grated lemon zest
- 1/3 c. roughly chopped red onion

DIRECTIONS

1. In a bowl, combine the salmon while using the beet horseradish, lemon zest, radish, capers, onions and chives, toss and serve cold.
2. Enjoy!

Nutritions: *Calories: 254 Fat:2 g, Carbs:7 g Protein:7 g Sugars:1.4 g Sodium:660 mg*

139. PARMESAN BAKED FISH

PREPARATION: 10 MIN

COOKING: 10 MIN

SERVES: 4

INGREDIENTS

- ½ tsp. Worcestershire sauce
- 1/3 c. mayonnaise
- 3 tbsps. Freshly grated parmesan cheese
- 4 oz. cod fish fillets
- 1 tbsp. snipped fresh chives

DIRECTIONS

1. Preheat oven to 450°C.
2. Rinse fish and pat dry with paper towels; spray an 8x8x2" baking dish with non-stick pan spray, set aside.
3. In small bowl stir mayo, grated cheese, chives, and Worcestershire sauce; spread mixture over fish fillets.
4. Bake, uncovered, 12-15 minutes or until fish flakes easily with a fork

Nutritions: *Calories:850.5 Fat: 24.8g Carbs:44.5 g Protein:104.6 g Sugars:0.6 g Sodium:307.7 mg*

140. SHRIMP AND MANGO MIX

PREPARATION: 10 MIN **COOKING: 10 MIN** **SERVES: 4**

INGREDIENTS

- 3 tbsps. Finely chopped parsley
- 3 tbsps. Coconut sugar
- 1 lb. peeled, deveined and cooked shrimp
- 6 tbsps. Avocado mayonnaise
- 3 tbsps. Balsamic vinegar
- 3 peeled and cubed mangos

DIRECTIONS

1. In a bowl, mix vinegar with sugar and mayo and whisk.
2. In another bowl, combine the mango with the parsley and shrimp, add the mayo mix, toss and serve.
3. Enjoy!

Nutritions: *Calories: 204 Fat: 3 g Carbs: 8 g Protein: 8 g Sugars: 12.6 g Sodium: 273.4 mg*

141. ROASTED HAKE

PREPARATION: 20 MIN

COOKING: 30 MIN

SERVES: 4

INGREDIENTS

- ½ c. tomato sauce
- 2 sliced tomatoes
- Fresh parsley
- ½ c. grated cheese
- 4 lbs. deboned hake fish
- 1 tbsp. olive oil
- Salt.

DIRECTIONS

1. Season the fish with salt. Pan-fry the fish until half-done.
2. Shape foil into containers according to the number of fish pieces.
3. Pour tomato sauce into each foil dish; arrange the fish, then the tomato slices, again add tomato sauce and sprinkle with grated cheese.
4. Bake in the oven at 400 F until there is a golden crust.
5. Serve with fresh parsley.

Nutritions: *Calories: 421 Fat:48.7 g Carbs:2.4 g Protein:17.4 g Sugars:0.5 g Sodium:94.6 mg*

142. COCONUT CREAM SHRIMP

PREPARATION: 10 MIN

COOKING: 20 MIN

SERVES: 2

INGREDIENTS

- 1 tbsp. coconut cream
- ½ tsp. lime juice
- ¼ tsp. black pepper
- 1 tbsp. parsley
- 1 lb. cooked, peeled and deveined shrimp
- ¼ tsp. chopped jalapeno

DIRECTIONS

1. In a bowl, mix the shrimp while using cream, jalapeno, lime juice, parsley and black pepper, toss, divide into small bowls and serve.
2. Enjoy!

Nutritions: *Calories: 183 Fat:5 g Carbs:12 g Protein:8 g Sugars:0.9 g Sodium:474.9 mg*

143. SIMPLE CINNAMON SALMON

PREPARATION: 10 MIN

COOKING: 10 MIN

SERVES: 2

INGREDIENTS

- 1 tbsp. organic essential olive oil
- Black pepper
- 1 tbsp. cinnamon powder
- 2 de-boned salmon fillets

DIRECTIONS

1. Heat up a pan with the oil over medium heat, add pepper and cinnamon and stir well.
2. Add salmon, skin side up, cook for 5 minutes on both sides, divide between plates and serve by using a side salad.
3. Enjoy!

Nutritions: *Calories: 220 Fat:8 g Carbs:11 g Protein:8 g Sugars:9.3 g Sodium:250.5 mg*

144. LEMON-HERB GRILLED FISH

PREPARATION: 5 MIN

COOKING: 10 MIN

SERVES: 4

INGREDIENTS

- 4 peeled garlic cloves
- ¼ tsp. salt
- 8 lemon slices
- ¼ tsp. ground black pepper
- Remoulade
- 2 small blue-fish
- 2 sprigs fresh thyme

DIRECTIONS

1. Prepare outdoor grill with medium-low to medium coals, or heat gas grill to medium-low to medium (to broil, see Note below).
2. Rinse fish; pat dry. Cut 3 slashes on each side. Season with salt, pepper.
3. Stuff 3 lemon slices in cavity of each fish. Add thyme and 2 cloves garlic to each cavity.
4. Grill fish 6 inches from heat, covered, 10 to 12 minutes, until just beginning to char. Flip over carefully. Cover each eye with one of remaining lemon slices. Grill 12 to 15 minutes more, until flesh is white throughout.
5. Transfer fish to platter. For each, pry up top fillet in one piece, flipping over, and skin side down.
6. Beginning at tail, carefully pull up end of spine of fish, and lift up, removing whole backbone. Remove any small bones from fish.
7. Serve with Remoulade.

Nutritions: *Calories: 118.1 Fat:6.8 g Carbs:1 g Protein:12.9 g Sugars:12.9 g Sodium:91.2 mg*

145. SCALLOPS AND STRAWBERRY MIX

PREPARATION: 20 MIN

COOKING: 30 MIN

SERVES: 2

INGREDIENTS

- 1 tbsp. lime juice
- ½ c. Pico de Gallo
- Black pepper
- 4 oz. scallops
- ½ c. chopped strawberries

DIRECTIONS

1. Heat up a pan over medium heat, add scallops, cook for 3 minutes on both sides and take away heat,
2. In a bowl, mix strawberries with lime juice, Pico de gallo, scallops and pepper, toss and serve cold.
3. Enjoy!

Nutritions: *Calories: 169 Fat:2 g Carbs:8 g Protein:13 g Sugars:0 g Sodium:235.7 mg*

146. COD PEAS RELISH

PREPARATION: 18-20 MIN   **COOKING: 40 MIN**   **SERVES: 4-5**

INGREDIENTS

- 1 c. peas
- 2 tbsps. Capers
- 4 de-boned medium cod fillets
- 3 tbsps. Olive oil
- ¼ tsp. black pepper
- 2 tbsps. Lime juice
- 2 tbsps. Chopped shallots
- 1 ½ tbsps. Chopped oregano

DIRECTIONS

1. Heat up 1 tbsp. olive oil in a saucepan over medium flame
2. Add the fillets, cook for 5 minutes on each side; set aside.
3. In a bowl of large size, thoroughly mix the oregano, shallots, lime juice, peas, capers, black pepper, and 2 tbsp. olive oil.
4. Toss and serve with the cooked fish.

Nutritions: *Calories: 224 Fat:11 g Carbs:7 g Protein:24 g Sugars:2 g Sodium:485 mg*

147. CHIPOTLE SPICED SHRIMP

PREPARATION: 10 MIN

COOKING: 10 MIN

SERVES: 4

INGREDIENTS

- ½ tsp. minced garlic
- 2 tbsps. Tomato paste
- ½ tsp. chopped fresh oregano
- 1 ½ tsps. Water
- ¾ lb. peeled, deveined and uncooked shrimp
- ½ tsp. chipotle chili powder
- ½ tsp. extra-virgin olive oil

DIRECTIONS

1. In cold water, rinse shrimp.
2. Pat dry with a paper towel. Set aside on a plate.
3. Whisk together the tomato paste, water and oil in a small bowl to make the marinade. Add garlic, chili powder and oregano and mix well.
4. Spread the marinade (it will be thick) on both sides of the shrimp using a brush and place in the refrigerator.
5. Heat a gas grill or broiler, or prepare a hot fire in a charcoal grill.
6. Coat the grill rack or broiler pan with cooking spray lightly.
7. Put the cooking rack 4 to 6 inches from the heat source.
8. Thread the shrimp onto skewers or lay them in a grill basket, to place on the grill.
9. After 3 to 4 minutes turn the shrimp.
10. When the shrimp is fully cooked, take it off the heat and serve immediately.

Nutritions: *Calories: 151.9 Fat:2.8 g Carbs:5.1 g Protein:24.2 g Sugars:2.3 g Sodium:283.1 mg*

148. BAKED HADDOCK

PREPARATION: 10 MIN

COOKING: 10 MIN

SERVES: 4

INGREDIENTS

- 1 tsp. chopped dill
- 3 tsps. Water
- ¼ tsp. black pepper and salt
- Cooking spray
- 1 lb. chopped haddock
- 2 tbsps. Fresh lemon juice
- 2 tbsps. Avocado mayonnaise

DIRECTIONS

1. Spray a baking dish with a few oils, add fish, water, freshly squeezed lemon juice, salt, black pepper, mayo and dill, toss, introduce inside the oven and bake at 350 0F for the half-hour.
2. Divide between plates and serve.
3. Enjoy!

Nutritions: *Calories: 264 Fat:4 g Carbs:7 g Protein:12 g Sugars:0 g Sodium:71.4 mg*

CHAPTER 10. SOUPS & STEWS RECIPES

149. SPRING VEGGIE SOUP

PREPARATION: 20 MIN

COOKING: 45 MIN

SERVES: 5

INGREDIENTS

- 2 tablespoons olive oil
- 1/2 cup onion, diced
- 1/2 cup mushrooms, sliced
- 1/8 cup celery, chopped
- 1 tomato, diced
- 1/2 cup carrots, diced
- 1 cup green beans, trimmed
- 1/2 cup frozen corn
- 1 teaspoon garlic powder
- 1 teaspoon dried oregano leaves
- 4 cups low-sodium vegetable broth

DIRECTIONS

1. In a pot, pour the olive oil and cook the onion and celery for 2 minutes.
2. Add the rest of the ingredients.
3. Bring to a boil.
4. Reduce heat and simmer for 45 minutes.

Nutritions: *Calories: 136 Fat: 11g Carbohydrates: 17g Protein: 7g Sodium: 138mg Potassium: 527mg Phosphorus: 125mg*

150. PESTO GREEN VEGETABLE SOUP

PREPARATION: 10 MIN

COOKING: 15 MIN

SERVES: 1

INGREDIENTS

- 2 teaspoons olive oil
- 1 sliced leek, white and light green
- 2 celery stalks, diced
- 1 teaspoon minced garlic
- 2 cups sodium-free chicken stock
- 1 cup chopped snow peas
- 1 cup shredded spinach
- 1 tablespoon chopped fresh thyme
- Juice and zest of ½ lemon
- ¼ teaspoon freshly ground black pepper
- 1 tablespoon Basil Pesto

DIRECTIONS

1. Add olive oil in a large saucepan.
2. Add the leek, celery, and garlic, and sauté until tender, about 3 minutes.
3. Stir in the stock and bring to a boil.
4. Stir in the snow peas, spinach, and thyme, and simmer for about 5 minutes.
5. Remove the pan from the heat, and stir in the lemon juice, lemon zest, pepper, and pesto.
6. Serve immediately.

Nutritions: *Calories: 170 Fat: 13g Carbohydrates: 8g Protein: 3g Sodium: 333mg Phosphorus: 42mg Potassium: 200mg*

151. EASY LOW-SODIUM CHICKEN BROTH

PREPARATION: 10 MIN

COOKING: 4 H

SERVES: 1

INGREDIENTS

- 2 pounds skinless whole chicken, cut into pieces
- 4 garlic cloves, lightly crushed
- 2 celery stalks, with greens, roughly chopped
- 2 carrots, roughly chopped
- 1 sweet onion, cut into quarters
- 10 peppercorns
- 4 fresh thyme sprigs
- 2 bay leaves
- Water

DIRECTIONS

1. In a large stockpot, place the chicken, garlic, celery, carrots, onion, peppercorns, thyme, and bay leaves, and cover with water by about 3 inches.
2. Let the water boil over high heat. Simmer for about 4 hours in low heat.
3. Skim off any foam on top of the stock and pour the stock through a fine-mesh sieve.
4. Pick off all the usable chicken meat for another recipe, discard the bones and other solids, and allow the stock to cool for about 30 minutes before transferring it to sealable containers.
5. You can put the stock in the refrigerator for 1 week or up to 2 months in the freezer.

Nutritions: *Calories: 32 Carbohydrates: 8g Protein: 1g Sodium: 57mg Potassium: 187mg Phosphorus: 50mg*

152. CREAM OF SPINACH SOUP

PREPARATION: 15 MIN

COOKING: 30 MIN

SERVES: 4

INGREDIENTS

- 1 tablespoon olive oil
- ½ sweet onion, chopped
- 2 teaspoons minced garlic
- 4 cups fresh spinach
- ¼ cup chopped fresh parsley
- 3 cups of water
- ¼ cup heavy (whipping) cream
- 1 tablespoon freshly squeezed lemon juice
- Freshly ground black pepper

DIRECTIONS

1. On a heated olive oil, sauté the onion and garlic in a large saucepan for 3 minutes.
2. Add the spinach and parsley, and sauté for 5 minutes.
3. Stir in the water, bring to a boil, then reduce the heat to low. Simmer the soup until the vegetables are tender, about 20 minutes.
4. Let it cool for 5 minutes, then, along with the heavy cream, purée the soup in batches in a food processor (or a blender or a handheld immersion blender).
5. Return the soup to the pot and cook through on low heat.
6. Add the lemon juice, season with pepper, and stir to combine. Serve hot.

Nutritions: *Calories: 141 Fat: 14g Carbohydrates: 3g Protein: 2g Sodium: 36mg Phosphorus: 38mg Potassium: 200mg*

153. VEGETABLE MINESTRONE

PREPARATION: 20 MIN   COOKING: 20 MIN   SERVES: 6

INGREDIENTS

- 1 teaspoon olive oil
- ½ sweet onion, chopped
- 1 celery stalk, diced
- 1 teaspoon minced garlic
- 2 cups sodium-free chicken stock
- 2 medium tomatoes, chopped
- 1 zucchini, diced
- ½ cup shredded stemmed kale
- Freshly ground black pepper
- 1-ounce grated Parmesan cheese

DIRECTIONS

1. Prepare a large saucepan over medium-high heat.
2. Add the onion, celery, and garlic. Sauté until softened, about 5 minutes.
3. Stir in the stock, tomatoes, and zucchini, and bring to a boil. Let it simmer for 15 minutes.
4. Stir in the kale and season with pepper.
5. Garnish with the parmesan cheese and serve.

Nutritions: *Calories: 100 Fat: 3g Carbohydrates: 6g Protein: 4g Sodium: 195mg Phosphorus: 70mg Potassium: 200mg*

154. VIBRANT CARROT SOUP

PREPARATION: 15 MIN

COOKING: 25 MIN

SERVES: 4

INGREDIENTS

- 1 tablespoon olive oil
- ½ sweet onion, chopped
- 2 teaspoons grated peeled fresh ginger
- 1 teaspoon minced fresh garlic
- 4 cups of water
- 3 carrots, chopped
- 1 teaspoon ground turmeric
- ½ cup of coconut milk
- 1 tablespoon chopped fresh cilantro

DIRECTIONS

1. Heat the olive oil in a saucepan.
2. Sauté the onion, ginger, and garlic until softened.
3. Stir in the water, carrots, and turmeric. Bring the soup to a boil, reduce the heat to low, and simmer until the carrots are tender about 20 minutes.
4. Transfer the soup in batches to a food processor (or blender) and process with the coconut milk until the soup is smooth.
5. Reheat the soup in a pan.
6. Serve topped with the cilantro.

Nutritions: *Calories: 113 Fat: 10g Protein: 1g Carbohydrates: 7g Sodium: 30mg Phosphorus: 50mg Potassium: 200mg;*

155. SIMPLE CABBAGE SOUP

PREPARATION: 20 MIN

COOKING: 35 MIN

SERVES: 8

INGREDIENTS

- 1 tablespoon olive oil
- ½ sweet onion, chopped
- 2 teaspoons minced garlic
- 6 cups of water
- 1 cup sodium-free chicken stock
- ½ head green cabbage, shredded
- 2 carrots, diced
- 2 medium tomatoes, diced
- Freshly ground black pepper
- 2 tablespoons chopped fresh thyme

DIRECTIONS

1. Prepare olive oil in a large saucepan over medium-high heat.
2. Sauté the onion and garlic until softened.
3. Add water, chicken stock, cabbage, carrots, and tomatoes. Let it bring it to a boil.
4. In medium-low heat, simmer the vegetables for 30 minutes or until tender.
5. Season the soup with black pepper. Serve hot, topped with the thyme.

Nutritions: *Calories: 62 Fat: 2g Carbohydrates: 6g Protein: 2g Sodium: 61mg Phosphorus: 32mg Potassium: 200mg*

156. MUSHROOM MOCK MISO SOUP

PREPARATION: 10 MIN   **COOKING: 35 MIN**   **SERVES: 6**

INGREDIENTS

- 6 cups water, divided
- 2 ounces dried mixed mushrooms
- ¼ cup of seasoned rice vinegar
- 1 teaspoon low-sodium soy sauce
- 1 tablespoon grated peeled fresh ginger
- 1 cup julienned snow peas
- ½ cup grated carrot
- 2 scallions, green and white parts, chopped

DIRECTIONS

1. Prepare 2 cups of water in a small saucepan over high heat and bring to a boil.
2. Place the dried mushrooms in a medium bowl and pour the boiling water over them. Let the mushrooms reconstitute for 30 minutes, then remove them from the water and slice them thinly.
3. Transfer the mushroom water, the remaining 4 cups of water, vinegar, soy sauce, ginger to a large saucepan, and place over medium-high heat.
4. Bring to a boil, then put mushrooms, snow peas, and carrot. Reduce the heat to low, and simmer for 5 minutes.
5. Serve hot, topped with the scallions.

Nutritions: *Calories: 56 Fat: 0g Carbohydrates: 9g Protein: 2g Sodium: 118mg Phosphorus: 43mg Potassium: 198mg*

157. FENNEL CAULIFLOWER SOUP

PREPARATION: 20 MIN   **COOKING: 30 MIN**   **SERVES: 1**

INGREDIENTS

- 1 teaspoon olive oil
- 1 small sweet onion, chopped
- 2 teaspoons minced garlic
- ½ small head cauliflower, cut into small florets
- 2 cups chopped fresh fennel
- 4 cups of water
- 2 teaspoons chopped fresh thyme
- ¼ cup heavy (whipping) cream

DIRECTIONS

1. Prepare a saucepan and heat the olive oil.
2. Put onion and garlic. Sauté until softened, about 3 minutes.
3. Add the cauliflower, fennel, and water. Let it boil, then reduce the heat to medium-low and simmer until the cauliflower is tender, about 20 minutes.
4. In batches, pour the soup into a food processor (or blender), and purée until smooth and creamy.
5. Return the soup to the pan. Stir in the thyme and cream—heat on medium-low until warmed through, about 5 minutes. Serve.

Nutritions: *Calories: 105 Fat: 8g Carbohydrates: 5g Protein: 1g Sodium: 30mg Phosphorus: 41mg Potassium: 200mg*

158. CHICKEN ALPHABET SOUP

PREPARATION: 15 MIN

COOKING: 35 MIN

SERVES: 6

INGREDIENTS

- 1 tablespoon olive oil
- ½ sweet onion, diced
- 2 teaspoons minced garlic
- 4 cups of water
- 1½ cups chopped cooked chicken breast
- 1 cup sodium-free chicken stock
- 2 celery stalks, chopped
- 1 carrot, peeled and diced
- ½ cup dried alphabet noodles
- Freshly ground black pepper
- 2 tablespoons chopped fresh parsley

DIRECTIONS

1. Put olive oil in a large saucepan with medium-high heat.
2. Add the onion and garlic. Cook until softened, about 3 minutes.
3. Add the water, chicken, chicken stock, celery, and carrot. Bring to a boil, then reduce the heat to medium-low and simmer until the vegetables are tender-crisp about 15 minutes.
4. Add the noodles, stir, and simmer the soup until the noodles are tender about 15 minutes.
5. Season with pepper. Serve hot with topped parsley.

Nutritions: *Calories: 132 Fat: 3g Carbohydrates: 10g Protein: 13g Sodium: 95mg Phosphorus: 116mg Potassium: 200mg*

159. MEATBALL SOUP

PREPARATION: 20 MIN   **COOKING: 40 MIN**   **SERVES: 6**

INGREDIENTS

- ½ pound lean ground beef
- 2 tablespoons breadcrumbs
- 1 tablespoon chopped fresh parsley
- 1 teaspoon minced garlic
- 1 teaspoon olive oil
- ½ sweet onion, chopped
- 5 cups of water
- 2 tomatoes, chopped
- 2 celery stalks with the greens, chopped
- 1 carrot, diced
- Freshly ground black pepper

DIRECTIONS

1. Mix the ground beef, breadcrumbs, parsley, and garlic in a large bowl. Roll the meat mixture into small (1-inch) meatballs.
2. Add the onion in a large saucepan, and sauté until softened, about 3 minutes.
3. Add the water, tomatoes, celery, and carrot, and bring to a boil. Add the meatballs, reduce the heat to medium-low, and simmer until the vegetables are tender and the meatballs are cooked through about 35 minutes.
4. Season the soup with pepper and serve hot.

Nutritions: *Calories: 106 Total fat: 3g Carbohydrates: 4g Protein: 9g Sodium: 53mg Phosphorus: 92mg Potassium: 200mg*

160. VEGETABLE STEW

PREPARATION: 15 MIN

COOKING: 15 MIN

SERVES: 8

INGREDIENTS

- 1 teaspoon olive oil
- 1 sweet onion, chopped
- 1 teaspoon minced garlic
- 2 zucchinis, chopped
- 1 red bell pepper, diced
- 2 carrots, chopped
- 2 cups low-sodium vegetable stock
- 2 large tomatoes, chopped
- 2 cups broccoli florets
- 1 teaspoon ground coriander
- ½ teaspoon ground cumin
- Pinch cayenne pepper
- Freshly ground black pepper
- 2 tablespoons chopped fresh cilantro

DIRECTIONS

1. Cook garlic and onion in a saucepan until softened.
2. Put zucchini, bell pepper, and carrots, and sauté for 5 minutes.
3. Mix vegetable stock, tomatoes, broccoli, coriander, cumin, and cayenne pepper.
4. Let it boil and simmer to medium-low until the vegetables are tender, often stirring about 5 minutes.
5. Add pepper and serve hot, topped with the cilantro.

Nutritions: *Calories: 45 Fat: 1g Carbohydrates: 5g Protein: 1g Sodium: 194mg Phosphorus: 21mg Potassium: 184mg*

161. PAPRIKA PORK SOUP

PREPARATION: 5 MIN

COOKING: 35 MIN

SERVES: 2

INGREDIENTS

- 4-ounce sliced pork loin
- 1 teaspoon black pepper
- 2 minced garlic cloves
- 1 cup baby spinach
- 3 cups water
- 1 tablespoon extra-virgin olive oil
- 1 chopped onion
- 1 tablespoon paprika

DIRECTIONS

1. Add in the oil, chopped onion and minced garlic.
2. Sauté for 5 minutes on low heat.
3. Add the pork slices to the onions and cook for 7-8 minutes or until browned.
4. Add the water to the pan and bring to a boil on high heat.
5. Stir in the spinach, reduce heat and simmer for a further 20 minutes or until pork is thoroughly cooked through.
6. Season with pepper to serve.

Nutritions: *Calories 165 Protein 13g Carbs 10g Fat 9g Sodium (Na) 269mg Potassium (K) 486mg Phosphorus 158mg*

162. MEDITERRANEAN VEGETABLE SOUP

PREPARATION: 5 MIN

COOKING: 30 MIN

SERVES: 4

INGREDIENTS

- 1 tablespoon oregano
- 2 minced garlic cloves
- 1 teaspoon black pepper
- 1 diced zucchini
- 1 cup diced eggplant
- 4 cups water
- 1 diced red pepper
- 1 tablespoon extra-virgin olive oil
- 1 diced red onion

DIRECTIONS

1. Soak the vegetables in warm water prior to use.
2. Add in the oil, chopped onion and minced garlic.
3. Sweat for 5 minutes on low heat.
4. Add the other vegetables to the onions and cook for 7-8 minutes.
5. Add the stock to the pan and bring to a boil on high heat.
6. Stir in the herbs, reduce the heat, and simmer for a further 20 minutes or until thoroughly cooked through.
7. Season with pepper to serve.

Nutritions: *Calories 152 Protein 1g Carbs 6g Fat 3g Sodium (Na) 3mg Potassium (K) 229mg Phosphorus 45mg*

163. TOFU SOUP

PREPARATION: 5 MIN

COOKING: 10 MIN

SERVES: 2

INGREDIENTS

- 1 tablespoon miso paste
- 1/8 cup cubed soft tofu
- 1 chopped green onion
- ¼ cup sliced shiitake mushrooms
- 3 cups renal stock
- 1 tablespoon soy sauce

DIRECTIONS

1. Take a saucepan, pour the stock into this pan and let it boil on high heat. Reduce heat to medium and let this stock simmer. Add mushrooms in this stock and cook for almost 3 minutes.
2. Take a bowl and mix soy sauce (reduced salt) and miso paste together in this bowl. Add this mixture and tofu in stock. Simmer for nearly 5 minutes and serve with chopped green onion.

Nutritions: *Calories 129 Fat 7.8g Sodium (Na) 484mg Potassium (K) 435mg Protein 11g Carbs 5.5g Phosphorus 73.2mg*

164. ONION SOUP

PREPARATION: 15 MIN

COOKING: 45 MIN

SERVES: 6

INGREDIENTS

- 2 tablespoons. Chicken stock
- 1 cup chopped shiitake mushrooms
- 1 tablespoon minced chives
- 3 teaspoons. Beef bouillon
- 1 teaspoon grated ginger root
- ½ chopped carrot
- 1 cup sliced portobello mushrooms
- 1 chopped onion
- ½ chopped celery stalk
- 2 quarts water
- ¼ teaspoon minced garlic

DIRECTIONS

1. Take a saucepan and combine carrot, onion, celery, garlic, mushrooms (some mushrooms) and ginger in this pan. Add water, beef bouillon and chicken stock in this pan. Put this pot on high heat and let it boil. Decrease flame to medium and cover this pan to cook for almost 45 minutes.
2. Put all remaining mushrooms in one separate pot. Once the boiling mixture is completely done, put one strainer over this new bowl with mushrooms and strain cooked soup in this pot over mushrooms. Discard solid-strained materials.
3. Serve delicious broth with yummy mushrooms in small bowls and sprinkle chives over each bowl.

Nutritions: *Calories 22 Fat 0g Sodium (Na) 602.3mg Potassium (K) 54.1mg Carbs 4.9g Protein 0.6g Phosphorus 15.8mg*

165. STEAKHOUSE SOUP

PREPARATION: 15 MIN

COOKING: 25 MIN

SERVES: 4

INGREDIENTS

- 2 tablespoons. Soy sauce
- 2 boneless and cubed chicken breasts.
- ¼ pound halved and trimmed snow peas
- 1 tablespoon minced ginger root
- 1 minced garlic clove
- 1 cup water
- 2 chopped green onions
- 3 cups chicken stock
- 1 chopped carrot
- 3 sliced mushrooms

DIRECTIONS

1. Take a pot and combine ginger, water, chicken stock, soy sauce (reduced salt) and garlic in this pot. Let them boil on medium heat, mix in chicken pieces, and let them simmer on low heat for almost 15 minutes to tender chicken.
2. Stir in carrot and snow peas and simmer for almost 5 minutes. Add mushrooms in this blend and continue cooking to tender vegetables for nearly 3 minutes. Mix in the chopped onion and serve hot.

Nutritions: *Calories 319 Carbs 14g Fat 15g Potassium (K) 225 Mg Protein 29g Sodium (Na) 389 Mg Phosphorous 190 Mg*

166. CHINESE-STYLE BEEF STEW

PREPARATION: 15 MIN

COOKING: 6-8 H

SERVES: 6

INGREDIENTS

- 2 medium carrots
- 2 green onions
- 2 celery stalks
- 1 medium green bell pepper, sliced
- 1 garlic clove
- 8 ounce of canned bean sprouts
- 8 ounce of canned water chestnuts
- 2 tablespoon of coconut oil
- 12ounce lean casserole beef, cut into cubes
- ½ cup low-sodium beef stock
- 1 tablespoon brown sugar
- 1/4 cup white wine vinegar
- 1 red chili, finely diced
- 1 ½ cups of water
- 3 cups cooked white rice

DIRECTIONS

1. Slice the carrots, green onions, celery and green pepper.
2. Crush the garlic. (hint: use the flat edge of a knife to do this easily.)
3. Rinse and slice the bamboo shoots and water chestnuts.
4. Heat the coconut oil and just brown the beef all over.
5. Transfer the beef to the slow cooker.
6. Add all the ingredients except the water.
7. Stir, it and then cover and cook on low for 6 to 8 hours.
8. Turn the slow cooker up to high.
9. Add the cold water to the slow cooker.
10. Stir it in to make it smooth, and leave the cooker lid slightly open.
11. Cook for a further 15 minutes.
12. Serve your dish over a bed of rice.

Nutritions: *Calories: 267 Protein: 14g Carbohydrates: 31g Fat: 9g Cholesterol: 35mg Sodium: 166mg Potassium: 319mg Phosphorus: 148mg Calcium: 41mg Fiber: 3g*

167. STUFFED BELL PEPPER SOUP

PREPARATION: 5 MIN   **COOKING: 20 MIN**   **SERVES: 2**

INGREDIENTS

- Chicken broth, low-sodium – 2 cups
- Bell pepper, red, diced – 1
- Garlic, minced – 4 cloves
- Onion, diced - .5 cup
- Ground turkey – 4 ounces
- Olive oil – 2 teaspoons
- Italian seasoning – 1 teaspoon
- White rice, cooked – 1 cup
- Parsley, fresh, chopped – 1 tablespoon

DIRECTIONS

1. Cook the ground turkey with the onion, olive oil, , and garlic until the turkey is fully cooked and no pink is remaining about five to seven minutes.
2. Add the black pepper, Italian seasoning, and bell pepper to the soup pot, allowing it to cook for three more minutes.
3. Into the pot, pour the low-sodium chicken broth, simmer the soup for fifteen minutes, until the bell peppers are tender. Stir in the cooked rice and parsley before serving.

Nutritions: *Calories 283 Protein Grams: 16 Phosphorus Milligrams: 183 Potassium Milligrams: 369 Sodium Milligrams: 85 Fat Grams: 9 Total Carbohydrates Grams: 32 Net Carbohydrates Grams: 30*

168. SALMON CHOWDER

PREPARATION: 20 MIN   **COOKING: 4 H**   **SERVES: 2**

INGREDIENTS

- 3 pounds salmon fillets, sliced into manageable pieces
- 1 1/2 cups onion, chopped
- 2 potatoes, cubed – limit this
- 3 cups water
- 1/3 teaspoon pepper
- 18-ounce evaporated milk, non-fat

DIRECTIONS

1. Put together onion, salmon, potatoes, and pepper in the slow cooker. Pour water
2. Cover and cook for 8 hours on low. Secure the lid.
3. After the 8-hour cooking cycle, turn off the heat. Adjust seasoning according to your preferred taste.
4. Stir in milk. Cover and cook for another 30 minutes. Serve right away.

Nutritions: *Protein: 33.8g Potassium: 204.3mg Sodium: 183.5 Mg*

169. BEEF STEW PASTA

PREPARATION: 15 MIN **COOKING: 8 H** **SERVES: 2**

INGREDIENTS

- 1 tablespoon olive oil
- 3/4-pound beef round roast, sliced into bite-sized pieces
- 1/2 cup onion, chopped
- 1/2 cup carrots, chopped
- 1/2 cup celery, chopped
- 2 cups beef broth, no salt
- 1/2 teaspoon oregano
- 1/4 cup red wine
- 1/4 teaspoon thyme
- 1/4 teaspoon black pepper
- 2 small tomatoes, diced – limit this
- 1/4 cup whole wheat pasta

DIRECTIONS

1. Pour olive oil into non-stick skillet. Cook beef round roast, in batches, for 5 minutes or until browned all over. Transfer meat to the slow cooker.
2. Add in onion, tomatoes, carrots, celery, beef broth, oregano, red wine, thyme, black pepper, and pasta. Stir mixture well.
3. Cover and cook for 8 to 9 hours on low. Secure the lid.
4. After the 8-hour cooking cycle, turn off the heat. Adjust seasoning according to your preferred taste.
5. To serve, place pasta into plates. Pour sauce all over.

Nutritions: *Protein: 12.8g Potassium: 128.5mg Sodium: 95.8mg*

170. ITALIAN CHICKEN STEW

PREPARATION: 20 MIN

COOKING: 8 H

SERVES: 1

INGREDIENTS

- 1/2-pound chicken breast, boneless, skinless, cubed
- 1/3 cup celery, chopped
- 1/2 cup carrot, chopped
- 1/2 cup onion, chopped
- 2 ounce any kind of mushrooms, sliced
- 1/4 teaspoon dill weed
- 1/2 teaspoon italian seasoning
- 1/4 teaspoon basil
- 1/4 teaspoon black pepper
- 1 tomato, diced – limit this

DIRECTIONS

1. Place chicken breast cubes into the slow cooker.
2. Add in onion, carrot, italian seasoning, mushrooms, celery, basil, dill weed, and black pepper. Add in diced tomatoes. Mix well.
3. Cover and cook for 8 to 9 hours on low. Secure the lid.
4. After the 8-hour cooking cycle, turn off the heat. Adjust seasoning according to your preferred taste.
5. Serve warm.

Nutritions: *Protein: 29.9g Potassium: 89.6mg Sodium: 56.3mg*

171. TURKEY PASTA STEW

PREPARATION: 10 MIN

COOKING: 8 H

SERVES: 1

INGREDIENTS

- 1/2-pound ground turkey
- 1/2 cup carrots, sliced
- 1/2 fennel bulb, chopped
- 1/4 cup celery, sliced
- 1 cup chicken broth, low sodium
- 1/3 teaspoon garlic, minced
- 1/2 teaspoon oregano
- 1/2 teaspoon basil
- 1/2 cup shell pasta, uncooked
- 1 cup navy beans, unsalted, cooked

DIRECTIONS

1. Cook turkey in a non-stick skillet set over medium heat until browned on all sides. Transfer to the slow cooker.
2. Add in garlic, carrots, chicken broth, navy beans, basil celery, pasta, oregano, and fennel. Stir well to combine.
3. Cover and cook for 8 to 9 hours on low. Secure the lid.
4. After the 8-hour cooking cycle, turn off the heat. Adjust seasoning according to your preferred taste. Serve warm.

Nutritions: *Protein: 18.8g Potassium: 84.6mg Sodium: 68.5mg*

172. ONE-POT CHICKEN PIE STEW

PREPARATION: 15 MIN   **COOKING: 1 H 15 MIN**   **SERVES: 8**

INGREDIENTS

- Fresh chicken breast (skinless and boneless) – 1½ pounds
- Low-sodium chicken stock – 2 cups
- Canola oil – ¼ cup
- Flour – ½ cup
- Fresh carrots (diced) – ½ cup
- Fresh onions (diced) – ½ cup
- Fresh celery (diced) – ¼ cup
- Black pepper – ½ teaspoon
- Italian seasoning (sodium-free) – 1 tablespoon
- Low-sodium better than bouillon® chicken base – 2 teaspoons
- Frozen sweet peas (thawed) – ½ cup
- Heavy cream – ½ cup
- Frozen piecrust (cooked, broken into bite-sized pieces) – 1
- Cheddar cheese (low-fat) – 1 cup

DIRECTIONS

1. Start by pounding the chicken to tenderize it. Cut into small equal-sized cubes.
2. Place it over a medium-high flame. Add in the stock and the chicken. Cook for about 30 minutes.
3. Add in the flour and oil, while the chicken is cooking, mix well to combine.
4. Stir the flour and oil mixture into the broth mixture. Keep stirring until the chicken broth starts to thicken.
5. Reduce the flame to low and cook for another 15 minutes.
6. Now add in the carrots, celery, onions, italian seasoning, bouillon, and black pepper. Cook for another 15 minutes.
7. Add in the cream and peas after turning off the flame. Keep stirring to mix well.
8. Transfer into soup mugs and top with the cheese and broken pie crust pieces.

Nutritions: *Protein 26g Carbohydrates 22g Fat 21g Cholesterol 82mg Sodium 424 Mg Potassium 209mg Phosphorus 290mg Calcium 88mg Fiber 2g*

RENAL DIET COOKBOOK FOR BEGINNERS

CHAPTER 11. SAUCE RECIPES

173. LEMON CAPER SAUCE

PREPARATION: 5 MIN   **COOKING: 7 MIN**   **SERVES: 6**

INGREDIENTS

- 2 tablespoons butter, unsalted
- 1 1/2 teaspoon all-purpose flour
- 1/2 cup reduced-sodium chicken broth
- 1/4 cup white wine
- 2 tablespoons lemon juice
- 1 teaspoon capers
- 1/4 teaspoon white pepper

DIRECTIONS

1. Set a suitable skillet over low heat and add the butter to melt.
2. Gradually stir in the flour and mix well for 1 minute.
3. Pour in the broth and continue mixing for another 1 minute.
4. Stir in the pepper, lemon juice, wine, capers, and lemon juice.
5. Mix well and cook by stirring for 5 minutes until it thickens.
6. Allow the sauce to cool down. Serve.

Nutritions: *Calories 48 Fat 4g Carbohydrate 0.9g Protein 0.6g Sodium 107mg Phosphorous 63mg Potassium 36mg*

174. ALFREDO SAUCE

PREPARATION: 5 MIN

COOKING: 5 MIN

SERVES: 4

INGREDIENTS

- 4 oz. cream cheese
- 1/2 cup grated Parmesan cheese
- 3/4 cup low-fat milk
- 1/4 cup butter
- 1/4 teaspoon white pepper
- 1/8 teaspoon garlic powder

DIRECTIONS

1. Set a 2-quart saucepan over moderate heat and add the Parmesan cheese, cream cheese, butter, milk, garlic powder, and white pepper.
2. Stir and cook this mixture for 5 minutes until the cheese is melted. Serve.

Nutritions: *Calories 311 Fat 27.8g Carbohydrate 4.2g Protein 12.8g Sodium 446mg Potassium 108mg Phosphorous 43mg*

175. BARBEQUE SAUCE

PREPARATION: 10 MIN   **COOKING: 20 MIN**   **SERVES: 8**

INGREDIENTS

- 1/3 cup corn oil
- 1/2 cup tomato juice
- 1 tablespoon brown Swerve
- 1 garlic clove
- 1 tablespoon paprika
- 1/4 cup vinegar
- 1 teaspoon pepper
- 1/3 cup water
- 1/4 teaspoon onion powder

DIRECTIONS

1. Toss all the ingredients into a suitable saucepan.
2. Cook this sauce for 20 minutes with occasional stirring. Serve.

Nutritions: *Calories 93 Fat 9.2g Carbohydrate 0.5g Protein 0.3g Sodium 42mg Potassium 68mg Phosphorous 31mg*

176. APPLE BUTTER

PREPARATION: 5 MIN

COOKING: 2 H

SERVES: 20

INGREDIENTS

- 4 1/2 cups apple sauce
- 2 cups granulated Swerve
- 1/4 cup vinegar
- 1/2 teaspoon ground cloves
- 1/2 teaspoon cinnamon

DIRECTIONS

1. Whisk the apple sauce, Swerve, vinegar, ground cloves, and cinnamon in a small roasting pan.
2. Bake the mixture for 2 hours at 350 degrees F in a preheated oven until it thickens.
3. Mix well and transfer to a mason jar.

Nutritions: *Calories 97 Fat 0g Carbohydrate 9.6g Protein 0.1g Sodium 1mg Potassium 40mg Phosphorous 110mg*

177. BLACKBERRY SAUCE

PREPARATION: 5 MIN

COOKING: 10 MIN

SERVES: 10

INGREDIENTS

- 5 cups blackberries
- 1/2 tablespoon stevia
- 1 tablespoon arrowroot powder
- 1 tablespoon lemon juice
- 1 cup water

DIRECTIONS

1. Crush the berries in a saucepan and add the stevia and a cup of water.
2. Bring the berries to a boil, then lower the heat to a simmer.
3. Whisk the arrowroot powder with 2 tablespoons of water in a bowl and add it to the berries.
4. Stir and cook the berries for 1 minute until the sauce thickens.
5. Remove the cooked berry sauce from heat and stir in lemon juice. Serve.

Nutritions: *Calories 60 Fat 0.4g Carbohydrate 14.8g Protein 1g Sodium 1mg Potassium 119mg Phosphorous 72mg*

178. BLUEBERRY SALSA

PREPARATION: 5 MIN

COOKING: 0 MIN

SERVES: 4

INGREDIENTS

- 1 cup blueberries
- 1 cup raspberries
- 1/4 cup red onion
- 2 tablespoons lime juice
- 1 tablespoon basil

DIRECTIONS

1. Add the berries, lime juice, onion, and basil to a food processor.
2. Pulse until all ingredients are finely chopped into a salsa.
3. Serve.

Nutritions: *Calories 45 Fat 0.4g Carbohydrate 11.5g Protein 0.8g Sodium 1mg Potassium 112mg Phosphorous 53mg*

179. CRANBERRY SALSA

PREPARATION: 5 MIN

COOKING: 0 MIN

SERVES: 4

INGREDIENTS

- 16 oz. canned whole cranberries, chopped
- 8 oz. canned pineapple, crushed
- 10 oz. frozen strawberries, chopped
- 1/2 cup apple sauce

DIRECTIONS

1. Toss the pineapple with the strawberries, cranberries, and apple sauce in a salad bowl.
2. Refrigerate the salsa for 2 hours or until ready to use.
3. Serve.

Nutritions: *Calories 127 Fat 0.1g Carbohydrate 29.3g Protein 0.9g Sodium 2.3mg Potassium 278mg Phosphorous 61mg*

180. STRAWBERRY SALSA

PREPARATION: 5 MIN

COOKING: 0 MIN

SERVES: 4

INGREDIENTS

- 1 1/2 cups strawberries
- 1/2 cup cucumber
- 1/2 cup red onion
- 2 tablespoons jalapeño pepper, halved and seeded
- 1 tablespoon mint
- 1 teaspoon lime rind
- 2 tablespoons lime juice
- 1 tablespoon orange juice
- 1 tablespoon honey

DIRECTIONS

1. Add the red onion, cucumber, strawberries, mint, and jalapeño to a food processor.
2. Pulse until all the ingredients are chopped into a salsa.
3. Add the lime juice, orange juice, honey, and mix well. Serve.

Nutritions: *Calories 49 Fat 0.2g Carbohydrate 13.2g Protein 0.8g Sodium 3mg Potassium 161mg Phosphorous 113mg*

181. GARLIC SAUCE

PREPARATION: 3 MIN

COOKING: 0 MIN

SERVES: 6

INGREDIENTS

- 1 garlic head, cloves peeled
- 2 tablespoons lemon juice
- 1 cup olive oil

DIRECTIONS

1. Add the garlic and lemon juice to a blender and blend to puree the garlic.
2. Slowly stir in the olive oil while blending the garlic mixture.
3. Serve.

Nutritions: *Calories 290 Fat 33.6g Carbohydrate 0.7g Protein 0.2g Sodium 1mg Potassium 14mg Phosphorous 20mg*

182. CRANBERRY SAUCE

PREPARATION: 3 MIN **COOKING: 10 MIN** **SERVES: 6**

INGREDIENTS

- 1 cup granulated Swerve
- 12 oz. whole cranberries
- 1 cup water

DIRECTIONS

1. Set a 2-quart saucepan over medium-high heat and add the Swerve and 1 cup water.
2. Bring the Swerve up to a boil, add the cranberries and reduce the heat to a simmer.
3. Cook, stirring gently for 10 minutes, then pass the mixture through a fine sieve over a mixing bowl.
4. Spread the berries in the sieve using the back of a spoon.
5. Mix well the strained sauce. Serve.

Nutritions: *Calories 25 Fat 0g Carbohydrate 7g Protein 0g Sodium 1mg Potassium 44mg Phosphorous 7mg*

CHAPTER 12. SNACKS AND SIDE DISHES

183. FLUFFY MOCK PANCAKES

PREPARATION: 5 MIN   **COOKING: 10 MIN**   **SERVES: 2**

INGREDIENTS

- 1 egg
- 1 cup ricotta cheese
- 1 teaspoon cinnamon
- 2 tablespoons honey, add more if needed

DIRECTIONS

1. Using a blender, put together egg, honey, cinnamon, and ricotta cheese. Process until all ingredients are well combined.
2. Pour an equal amount of the blended mixture into the pan. Cook each pancake for 4 minutes on both sides. Serve.

Nutritions: *Calories: 188.1 Kcal Total Fat: 14.5g Saturated Fat: 4.5g Cholesterol: 139.5mg Sodium: 175.5mg Total Carbs: 5.5g Fiber: 2.8g Sugar: 0.9g Protein: 8.5g*

184. MIXES OF SNACK

PREPARATION: 10 MIN

COOKING: 1 H 15 MIN

SERVES: 4

INGREDIENTS

- 6 cup margarine
- 2 tablespoon Worcestershire sauce
- 1 ½ tablespoon spice salt
- ¾ cup garlic powder
- ½ teaspoon onion powder
- 3 cups crispi
- 3 cups cheerios
- 3 cups corn flakes
- 1 cup kixe
- 1 cup pretzels
- 1 cup broken bagel chips into 1-inch pieces

DIRECTIONS

1. Preheat the oven to 250f (120c)
2. Melt the margarine in a pan. Stir in the seasoning. Gradually add the ingredients remaining by mixing so that the coating is uniform.
3. Cook 1 hour, stirring every 15 minutes. Spread on paper towels to let cool. Store in a tightly-closed container.

Nutritions: *Calories: 200 Kcal Total Fat: 9g Saturated Fat: 3.5g Cholesterol: 0mg Sodium: 3.5mg Total Carbs: 27g Fiber: 2g Sugar: 0g Protein: 3g*

185. CRANBERRY DIP WITH FRESH FRUIT

PREPARATION: 10 MIN

COOKING: 0 MIN

SERVES: 8

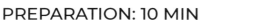

INGREDIENTS

- 8-ounce sour cream
- 1/2 cup whole berry cranberry sauce
- 1/4 teaspoon nutmeg
- 1/4 teaspoon ground ginger
- 4 cups fresh pineapple, peeled, cubed
- 4 medium apples, peeled, cored and cubed
- 4 medium pears, peeled, cored and cubed
- 1 teaspoon lemon juice

DIRECTIONS

1. Start by adding cranberry sauce, sour cream, ginger, and nutmeg to a food processor.
2. Blend the mixture until its smooth then transfer it to a bowl.
3. Toss the pineapple, with pears, apples, and lemon juice in a salad bowl.
4. Thread the fruits onto mini skewers.
5. Serve them with the sauce.

Nutritions: *Calories 70 Protein 0g Carbohydrates 13g Fat 2g Cholesterol 4mg Sodium 8mg Potassium 101 Mg Phosphorus 15mg Calcium 17mg Fiber 1.5g*

186. CUCUMBERS WITH SOUR CREAM

PREPARATION: 10 MIN

COOKING: 0 MIN

SERVES: 4

INGREDIENTS

- 2 medium cucumbers, peeled and sliced thinly
- 1/2 medium sweet onion, sliced
- 1/4 cup white wine vinegar
- 1 tablespoon canola oil
- 1/8 teaspoon black pepper
- 1/2 cup reduced-fat sour cream

DIRECTIONS

1. Toss in cucumber, onion, and all other ingredients in a medium-size bowl.
2. Mix well and refrigerate for 2 hours.
3. Toss again and serve to enjoy.

Nutritions: *Calories 64. Protein 1g Carbohydrates 4g Fat 5g Cholesterol 3mg Sodium 72mg Potassium 113mg Phosphorus 24mg Calcium 21mg Fiber 0.8g*

187. SWEET SAVORY MEATBALLS

PREPARATION: 10 MIN   **COOKING: 20 MIN**   **SERVES: 12**

INGREDIENTS

- 1-pound ground turkey
- 1 large egg
- 1/4 cup bread crumbs
- 2 tablespoon onion, finely chopped
- 1 teaspoon garlic powder
- 1/2 teaspoon black pepper
- 1/4 cup canola oil
- 6-ounce grape jelly
- 1/4 cup chili sauce

DIRECTIONS

1. Place all ingredients except chili sauce and jelly in a large mixing bowl.
2. Mix well until evenly mixed then make small balls out of this mixture.
3. It will make about 48 meatballs. Spread them out on a greased pan on a stovetop.
4. Cook them over medium heat until brown on all the sides.
5. Mix chili sauce with jelly in a microwave-safe bowl and heat it for 2 minutes in the microwave.
6. Pour this chili sauce mixture onto the meatballs in the pan.
7. Transfer the meatballs in the pan to the preheated oven.
8. Bake the meatballs for 20 minutes in an oven at 375 degrees f.
9. Serve fresh and warm.

Nutritions: *Calories 127 Protein 9g Carbohydrates 14g Fat 4g Cholesterol 41mg Sodium 129mg Potassium 148mg Phosphorus 89mg Calcium 15mg Fiber 0.2g.*

188. SPICY CORN BREAD

PREPARATION: 10 MIN

COOKING: 30 MIN

SERVES: 8

INGREDIENTS

- 1 cup all-purpose white flour
- 1 cup plain cornmeal
- 1 tablespoon sugar
- 2 teaspoon baking powder
- 1 teaspoon chili powder
- 1/4 teaspoon black pepper
- 1 cup rice milk, unenriched
- 1 egg
- 1 egg white
- 2 tablespoon canola oil
- 1/2 cup scallions, finely chopped
- 1/4 cup carrots, finely grated
- 1 garlic clove, minced

DIRECTIONS

1. Preheat your oven to 400 degrees f.
2. Now start by mixing the flour with baking powder, sugar, cornmeal, pepper and chili powder in a mixing bowl.
3. Stir in oil, milk, egg white, and egg.
4. Mix well until it's smooth then stir in carrots, garlic, and scallions.
5. Stir well then spread the batter in an 8-inch baking pan greased with cooking spray.
6. Bake for 30 minutes until golden brown.
7. Slice and serve fresh.

Nutritions: *Calories 188 Protein 5g Carbohydrates 31g Fat 5g Cholesterol 26mg Sodium 155mg Potassium 100mg Phosphorus 81mg Calcium 84mg Fiber 2g*

189. SWEET AND SPICY TORTILLA CHIPS

PREPARATION: 10 MIN

COOKING: 8 MIN

SERVES: 6

INGREDIENTS

- 1/4 cup butter
- 1 teaspoon brown sugar
- 1/2 teaspoon ground chili powder
- 1/2 teaspoon garlic powder
- 1/2 teaspoon ground cumin
- 1/4 teaspoon ground cayenne pepper
- 6 flour tortillas, 6" size

DIRECTIONS

1. Preheat oven to 425 degrees f.
2. Grease a baking sheet with cooking spray.
3. Add all spices, brown sugar, and melted butter to a small bowl.
4. Mix well and set this mixture aside.
5. Slice the tortillas into 8 wedges and brush them with the sugar mixture.
6. Spread them on the baking sheet and bake them for 8 minutes.
7. Serve fresh.

Nutritions: *Calories 115 Protein 2g Carbohydrates 11g Fat 7g Cholesterol 15mg Sodium 156mg Potassium 42mg Phosphorus 44mg Calcium 31mg Fiber 0.6g*

190. ADDICTIVE PRETZELS

PREPARATION: 10 MIN

COOKING: 1 H

SERVES: 6

INGREDIENTS

- 32-ounce bag unsalted pretzels
- 1 cup canola oil
- 2 tablespoon seasoning mix
- 3 teaspoon garlic powder
- 3 teaspoon dried dill weed

DIRECTIONS

1. Preheat oven to 175 degrees f.
2. Place the pretzels on a cooking sheet and break them into pieces.
3. Mix garlic powder and dill in a bowl and reserve half of the mixture.
4. Mix the remaining half with seasoning mix and ¾ cup of canola oil.
5. Pour this oil over the pretzels and brush them liberally
6. Bake the pieces for 1 hour then flip them to bake for another 15 minutes.
7. Allow them to cool then sprinkle the remaining dill mixture and drizzle more oil on top.
8. Serve fresh and warm.

Nutritions: *Calories 184 Protein 2g Carbohydrates 22g Fat 8g Cholesterol 0mg Sodium 60mg Potassium 43mg Phosphorus 28mg Calcium 2mg Fiber 1.0g*

191. SHRIMP SPREAD WITH CRACKERS

PREPARATION: 10 MIN

COOKING: 0 MIN

SERVES: 6

INGREDIENTS

- 1/4 cup light cream cheese
- 2 1/2-ounce cooked, shelled shrimp, minced
- 1 tablespoon no-salt-added ketchup
- 1/4 teaspoon hot sauce
- 1 teaspoon worcestershire sauce
- 1/2 teaspoon herb seasoning blend
- 24 matzo cracker miniatures
- 1 tablespoon parsley

DIRECTIONS

1. Start by tossing the minced shrimp with cream cheese in a bowl.
2. Stir in worcestershire sauce, hot sauce, herb seasoning, and ketchup.
3. Mix well and garnish with minced parsley.
4. Serve the spread with the crackers.

Nutritions: *Calories 57 Protein 3g Carbohydrates 7g Fat 1g Cholesterol 21mg Sodium 69mg Potassium 54mg Phosphorus 30mg Calcium 15mg Fiber 0.2g*

192. BUFFALO CHICKEN DIP

PREPARATION: 10 MIN

COOKING: 3 H

SERVES: 4

INGREDIENTS

- 4-ounce cream cheese
- 1/2 cup bottled roasted red peppers
- 1 cup reduced-fat sour cream
- 4 teaspoon hot pepper sauce
- 2 cups cooked, shredded chicken

DIRECTIONS

1. Blend half cup of drained red peppers in a food processor until smooth.
2. Now, thoroughly mix cream cheese, and sour cream with the pureed peppers in a bowl.
3. Stir in shredded chicken and hot sauce then transfer the mixture to a slow cooker.
4. Cook for 3 hours on low heat.
5. Serve warm with celery, carrots, cauliflower, and cucumber.

Nutritions: *Calories 73 Protein 5g Carbohydrates 2g Fat 5g Cholesterol 25mg Sodium 66mg Potassium 81mg Phosphorus 47mg Calcium 31mg Fiber 0g*

193. CHICKEN PEPPER BACON WRAPS

PREPARATION: 10 MIN   **COOKING: 15 MIN**   **SERVES: 4**

INGREDIENTS

- 1 medium onion, chopped
- 12 strips bacon, halved
- 12 fresh jalapenos peppers
- 12 fresh banana peppers
- 2 pounds boneless, skinless chicken breast

DIRECTIONS

1. Grease a grill rack with cooking spray and preheat the grill on low heat.
2. Slice the peppers in half lengthwise then remove their seeds.
3. Dice the chicken into small pieces and divide them into each pepper.
4. Now spread the chopped onion over the chicken in the peppers.
5. Wrap the bacon strips around the stuffed peppers.
6. Place these wrapped peppers in the grill and cook them for 15 minutes.
7. Serve fresh and warm.

Nutritions: *Calories 71 Protein 10g Carbohydrates 1g Fat 3g Cholesterol 26mg Sodium 96mg Potassium 147mg Phosphorus 84mg Calcium 9mg.fiber 0.8g*

194. GARLIC OYSTER CRACKERS

PREPARATION: 10 MIN

COOKING: 45 MIN

SERVES: 4

INGREDIENTS

- 1/2 cup butter-flavored popcorn oil
- 1 tablespoon garlic powder
- 7 cups oyster crackers
- 2 teaspoon dried dill weed

DIRECTIONS

1. Preheat oven to 250 degrees f.
2. Mix garlic powder with oil in a large bowl.
3. Toss in crackers and mix well to coat evenly.
4. Sprinkle the dill weed over the crackers and toss well again.
5. Spread the crackers on the baking sheet and bake them for 45 minutes.
6. Toss them every 15 minutes.
7. Serve fresh.

Nutritions: *Calories 118 Protein 2g Carbohydrates 12g Fat 7g Cholesterol 0mg Sodium 166mg Potassium 21mg Phosphorus 15mg Calcium 4mg Fiber 3g*

195. LIME CILANTRO RICE

PREPARATION: 5 MIN   **COOKING: 20 MIN**   **SERVES: 2**

INGREDIENTS

- White rice – .75 cup
- Water – 1.5 cups
- Olive oil – 1.5 tablespoons
- Bay leaf, ground - .25 teaspoon
- Lime juice – 1 tablespoon
- Lemon juice – 1 tablespoon
- Lime zest - .25 teaspoon
- Cilantro, chopped - .25 cup

DIRECTIONS

1. Place the white rice and water in a medium-sized saucepan and bring it to a boil over medium heat. Simmer and cover the pot with a lid, allowing it to cook until all water has been absorbed about eighteen to twenty minutes.
2. Stir in the ground bay leaf, olive oil, lime juice, lemon juice, lime zest, and cilantro after cooking. You want to do this with a fork, preferably, as this will fluff the rice rather than causing it to compact. Serve while warm.

Nutritions: *Calories 363 Protein Grams: 5 Phosphorus Milligrams: 74 Potassium Milligrams: 86 Sodium Milligrams: 5 Fat Grams: 10 Total Carbohydrates Grams: 60 Net Carbohydrates Grams: 58*

196. GINGER CAULIFLOWER RICE

PREPARATION: 10 MIN   **COOKING: 10 MIN**   **SERVES: 4**

INGREDIENTS

- 5 cups cauliflower florets
- 3 tablespoons coconut oil
- 4 ginger slices, grated
- 1 tablespoon coconut vinegar
- 3 garlic cloves, minced
- 1 tablespoon chives, minced
- A pinch of sea salt
- Black pepper to taste

DIRECTIONS

1. Put cauliflower florets in a food processor and pulse well.
2. Heat up a pan with the oil over medium-high heat, add ginger, stir and cook for 3 minutes.
3. Add cauliflower rice and garlic, stir and cook for 7 minutes.
4. Add salt, black pepper, vinegar, and chives, stir, cook for a few seconds more, divide between plates and serve.
5. Enjoy!

Nutritions: *Calories 125 fat 10,4 fiber 3,2 carbs 7,9 protein 2,7 Phosphorus: 110mg Potassium: 117mg Sodium: 75mg*

197. BASIL ZUCCHINI SPAGHETTI

PREPARATION: 1 H 10 MIN **COOKING: 10 MIN** **SERVES: 4**

INGREDIENTS

- 1/3 cup coconut oil, melted
- 4 zucchinis, cut with a spiralizer
- ¼ cup basil, chopped
- A pinch of sea salt
- Black pepper to taste
- ½ cup walnuts, chopped
- 2 garlic cloves, minced

DIRECTIONS

1. In a bowl, mix zucchini spaghetti with salt and pepper, toss to coat, leave aside for 1 hour, drain well and put in a bowl.
2. Heat up a pan with the oil over medium-high heat, add zucchini spaghetti and garlic, stir and cook for 5 minutes.
3. Add basil and walnuts and black pepper, stir and cook for 3 minutes more.
4. Divide between plates and serve as a side dish
5. Enjoy!

Nutritions: *Calories 287 Fat 27,8 Fiber 3,3 Carbs 8,7 Protein 6,3 Phosphorus: 110mg Potassium: 117mg Sodium: 75mg*

198. BRAISED CABBAGE

PREPARATION: 10 MIN

COOKING: 10 MIN

SERVES: 4

INGREDIENTS

- 1 small cabbage head, shredded
- 2 tablespoons water
- A drizzle of olive oil
- 6 ounces shallots, cooked and chopped
- A pinch of black pepper
- A pinch of sweet paprika
- 1 tablespoon dill, chopped

DIRECTIONS

1. Heat up a pan with the oil over medium heat, add the cabbage and the water, stir and sauté for 5 minutes.
2. Add the rest of the ingredients, toss, cook for 5 minutes more, divide everything between plates and serve as a side dish!
3. Enjoy!

Nutritions: *Calories 91 Fat 0,5 Fiber 5,8 Carbs 20,8 Protein 4,1 Phosphorus: 120mg Potassium: 127mg Sodium: 75mg*

199. CAULIFLOWER AND LEEKS

PREPARATION: 10 MIN

COOKING: 20 MIN

SERVES: 4

INGREDIENTS

- 1 and ½ cups leeks, chopped
- 1 and ½ cups cauliflower florets
- 2 garlic cloves, minced
- 1 and ½ cups artichoke hearts
- 2 tablespoons coconut oil, melted
- Black pepper to taste

DIRECTIONS

1. Heat up a pan with the oil over medium-high heat, add garlic, leeks, cauliflower florets and artichoke hearts, stir and cook for 20 minutes.
2. Add black pepper, stir, divide between plates and serve.
3. Enjoy!

Nutritions: *Calories 192 Fat 6,9 Fiber 8,2 Carbs 35,1 Protein 5,1 Phosphorus: 110mg Potassium: 117mg Sodium: 75mg*

200. EGGPLANT AND MUSHROOM SAUTÉ

PREPARATION: 10 MIN   **COOKING: 30 MIN**   **SERVES: 4**

INGREDIENTS

- 2 pounds oyster mushrooms, chopped
- 6 ounces shallots, peeled, chopped
- 1 yellow onion, chopped
- 2 eggplants, cubed
- 3 celery stalks, chopped
- 1 tablespoon parsley, chopped
- A pinch of sea salt
- Black pepper to taste
- 1 tablespoon savory, dried
- 3 tablespoons coconut oil, melted

DIRECTIONS

1. Heat up a pan with the oil over medium high heat, add onion, stir and cook for 4 minutes.
2. Add shallots, stir and cook for 4 more minutes.
3. Add eggplant pieces, mushrooms, celery, savory and black pepper to taste, stir and cook for 15 minutes.
4. Add parsley, stir again, cook for a couple more minutes, divide between plates and serve.
5. Enjoy!

Nutritions: *Calories 1013 Fat 10,9 Fiber 35,5 Carbs 156,5 Protein 69,1 Phosphorus: 210mg Potassium: 217mg Sodium: 105mg*

201. MINT ZUCCHINI

PREPARATION: 10 MIN

COOKING: 7 MIN

SERVES: 4

INGREDIENTS

- 2 tablespoons mint
- 2 zucchinis, halved lengthwise and then slice into half moons
- 1 tablespoon coconut oil, melted
- ½ tablespoon dill, chopped
- A pinch of cayenne pepper

DIRECTIONS

1. Heat up a pan with the oil over medium-high heat, add zucchinis, stir and cook for 6 minutes.
2. Add cayenne, dill and mint, stir, cook for 1 minute more, divide between plates and serve.
3. Enjoy!

Nutritions: *Calories 46 Fat 3,6 Fiber 1,3 Carbs 3,5 Protein 1,3 Phosphorus: 120mg Potassium: 127mg Sodium: 75mg*

202. CELERY AND KALE MIX

PREPARATION: 10 MIN

COOKING: 20 MIN

SERVES: 4

INGREDIENTS

- 2 celery stalks, chopped
- 5 cups kale, torn
- 1 small red bell pepper, chopped
- 3 tablespoons water
- 1 tablespoon coconut oil, melted

DIRECTIONS

1. Heat up a pan with the oil over medium-high heat, add celery, stir and cook for 10 minutes.
2. Add kale, water, and bell pepper, stir and cook for 10 minutes more.
3. Divide between plates and serve.
4. Enjoy!

Nutritions: *Calories 81 Fat 3,5 Fiber 1,8 Carbs 11,3 Protein 2,9 Phosphorus: 120mg Potassium: 147mg Sodium: 75mg*

203 KALE, MUSHROOMS AND RED CHARD MIX

PREPARATION: 10 MIN

COOKING: 17 MIN

SERVES: 4

INGREDIENTS

- ½ pound brown mushrooms, sliced
- 5 cups kale, roughly chopped
- 1 and ½ tablespoons coconut oil
- 3 cups red chard, chopped
- 2 tablespoons water
- Black pepper to taste

DIRECTIONS

1. Heat up a pan with the oil over medium high heat, add mushrooms, stir and cook for 5 minutes.
2. Add red chard, kale and water, stir and cook for 10 minutes.
3. Add black pepper to taste, stir and cook 2 minutes more.
4. Divide between plates and serve.
5. Enjoy!

Nutritions: *Calories 97 Fat 3,4 Fiber 2,3 Carbs 13,3 Protein 5,4 Phosphorus: 110mg Potassium: 117mg Sodium: 75mg*

204. BOK CHOY AND BEETS

PREPARATION: 10 MIN

COOKING: 30 MIN

SERVES: 4

INGREDIENTS

- 1 tablespoon coconut oil
- 4 cups bok choy, chopped
- 3 beets, cut into quarters and thinly sliced
- 2 tablespoons water
- A pinch of cayenne pepper

DIRECTIONS

1. Put water in a large saucepan, add the beets, bring to a boil over medium heat, cover, cook for 20 minutes and drain.
2. Heat up a pan with the oil over medium high heat, add the bok choy and the water, stir and cook for 10 minutes.
3. Add beets and cayenne pepper, stir, cook for 2 minutes more, divide between plates and serve as a side dish!
4. Enjoy!

Nutritions: *Calories 71 Fat 3,7 Fiber 2,2 Carbs 9 Protein 2,3 Phosphorus: 110mg Potassium: 117mg Sodium: 75mg*

205. SPICY SWEET POTATOES

PREPARATION: 10 MIN

COOKING: 40 MIN

SERVES: 2

INGREDIENTS

- 4 sweet potatoes, peeled and thinly sliced
- 2 teaspoons nutmeg, ground
- 2 tablespoon coconut oil, melted
- Cayenne pepper to taste

DIRECTIONS

1. In a bowl, mix sweet potato slices with nutmeg, cayenne, and oil and toss to coat well.
2. Spread these on a lined baking sheet, place in the oven at 350 degrees F and bake for 25 minutes.
3. Flip the potatoes, bake for 15 minutes more, divide between plates and serve as a side dish.
4. Enjoy!

Nutritions: *Calories 242 Fat 7,5 Fiber 6,4 Carbs 42,4 Protein 2,4 Phosphorus: 120mg Potassium: 137mg Sodium: 75mg*

206. BROCCOLI AND ALMONDS MIX

PREPARATION: 10 MIN

COOKING: 11 MIN

SERVES: 4

INGREDIENTS

- 1 tablespoon olive oil
- 1 garlic clove, minced
- 1 pound broccoli florets
- 1/3 cup almonds, chopped
- Black pepper to taste

DIRECTIONS

1. Heat up a pan with the oil over medium-high heat, add the almonds, stir, cook for 5 minutes and transfer to a bowl,
2. Heat up the same pan again over medium-high heat, add broccoli and garlic, stir, cover and cook for 6 minutes more.
3. Add the almonds and black pepper to taste, stir, divide between plates and serve.
4. Enjoy!

Nutritions: *Calories 116 Fat 7,8 Fiber 4 Carbs 9,5 Protein 4,9 Phosphorus: 110mg Potassium: 117mg Sodium: 75mg*

207. SQUASH AND CRANBERRIES

PREPARATION: 10 MIN **COOKING: 30 MIN** **SERVES: 2**

INGREDIENTS

- 1 tablespoon coconut oil
- 1 butternut squash, peeled and cubed
- 2 garlic cloves, minced
- 1 small yellow onion, chopped
- 12 ounces coconut milk
- 1 teaspoon curry powder
- 1 teaspoon cinnamon powder
- ½ cup cranberries

DIRECTIONS

1. Spread squash pieces on a lined baking sheet, place in the oven at 425 degrees F, bake for 15 minutes and leave to one side.
2. Heat up a pan with the oil over medium high heat, add garlic and onion, stir and cook for 5 minutes.
3. Add roasted squash, stir and cook for 3 minutes.
4. Add coconut milk, cranberries, cinnamon and curry powder, stir and cook for 5 minutes more.
5. Divide between plates and serve as a side dish!
6. Enjoy!

Nutritions: *Calories 518 Fat 47,6 Fiber 7,3 Carbs 24,9 Protein 5,3 Phosphorus: 110mg Potassium: 117mg Sodium: 75mg*

208. CREAMY CHARD

PREPARATION: 10 MIN

COOKING: 10 MIN

SERVES: 2

INGREDIENTS

- Juice of ½ lemon
- 1 tablespoon coconut oil
- 12 ounces coconut milk
- 1 bunch chard
- A pinch of sea salt
- Black pepper to taste

DIRECTIONS

1. Heat up a pan with the oil over medium-high heat, add chard, stir and cook for 5 minutes.
2. Add lemon juice, a pinch of salt, black pepper, and coconut milk, stir and cook for 5 minutes more.
3. Divide between plates and serve as a side.
4. Enjoy!

Nutritions: *Calories 453 Fat 47,4 Fiber 4 Carbs 10,1 Protein 4,2 Phosphorus: 130mg Potassium: 1127mg Sodium: 85mg*

209. DILL CARROTS

PREPARATION: 10 MIN

COOKING: 30 MIN

SERVES: 4

INGREDIENTS

- 1 tablespoon coconut oil, melted
- 2 tablespoons dill, chopped
- 1 pound baby carrots
- 1 tablespoon coconut sugar
- A pinch of black pepper

DIRECTIONS

1. Put carrots in a large saucepan, add water to cover, bring to a boil over medium-high heat, cover and simmer for 30 minutes.
2. Drain the carrots, put them in a bowl, add melted oil, black pepper, dill, and the coconut sugar, stir very well, divide between plates and serve.
3. Enjoy!

Nutritions: *Calories 85 Fat 3,6 Fiber 3,5 Carbs 13,4 Protein 1 Phosphorus: 140mg Potassium: 147mg Sodium: 65mg*

CHAPTER 13. SMOOTHIES AND DRINKS

210. RASPBERRY CUCUMBER SMOOTHIE

PREPARATION: 5 MIN

COOKING: 5 MIN

SERVES: 2

INGREDIENTS

- 1 c. fresh or frozen raspberries
- ½ c. diced English cucumber
- 1 c. Homemade Rice Milk (or use unsweetened store-bought) or almond milk
- 2 tsp. chia seeds
- 1 tsp. honey
- 3 ice cubes

DIRECTIONS

1. Place the raspberries, cucumber, rice milk, chia seeds, and honey in a blender. Then, blend until smooth.
2. Add the ice cubes. Then, blend until thick and smooth.
3. Pour into two tall glasses. Serve immediately.

Nutritions: *Calories: 125 Fat: 1.1g Carbs: 23.5g Protein: 6g Sodium: 44mg Potassium: 199mg Phosphorus: 54mg*

211. MANGO CHEESECAKE SMOOTHIE

PREPARATION: 5 MIN

COOKING: 5 MIN

SERVES: 2

INGREDIENTS

- 1 c. Homemade Rice Milk
- ½ ripe fresh mango, peeled and chopped
- 2 tbsp. cream cheese, at room temperature
- 1 tsp. honey
- ½ vanilla bean split and seeds scraped out
- Pinch ground nutmeg
- 3 ice cubes

DIRECTIONS

1. Place the rice milk, mango, cream cheese, honey, vanilla bean seeds, and nutmeg in a blender, and blend until smooth and thick.
2. Add the ice cubes and blend.
3. Serve in two glasses immediately.

Nutritions: *Calories: 177 Fat: 4g Carbs: 10g Protein: 24g Sodium: 346mg Potassium: 66mg Phosphorus: 62mg*

212. HOT COCOA

 PREPARATION: 5 MIN

 COOKING: 5 MIN

 SERVES: 1

INGREDIENTS

- 1 tbsp. cocoa powder, unsweetened
- 2 tsp. Splenda granulated sugar
- 3 tbsp. whipped dessert topping
- 1 c. water, at room temperature
- 2 tbsp. water, cold

DIRECTIONS

1. Place a saucepan over medium heat and let it heat until hot.
2. Take a cup, place cocoa powder and sugar in it, pour in cold water, and mix well.
3. Then slowly stir in hot water until cocoa mixture dissolves and top with whipped topping.
4. Serve straight away.

Nutritions: *Calories: 120 Fat: 3g Carbs: 23g Protein: 1g Sodium: 110mg Potassium: 199mg Phosphorus: 88mg*

213. RICE MILK

PREPARATION: 2 MIN

COOKING: 2 MIN

SERVES: 2

INGREDIENTS

- 1 c. rice milk, unenriched, chilled
- 1 scoop vanilla whey protein

DIRECTIONS

1. Pour milk in a blender, add whey protein, and then pulse until well blended.
2. Distribute the milk into two glasses and serve.

Nutritions: *Calories: 120 Fat: 2g Carbs: 24g Protein: 0g Sodium: 86mg Potassium: 27mg Phosphorus: 56mg*

214. ALMOND MILK

PREPARATION: 3 MIN

COOKING: 2 MIN

SERVES: 3

INGREDIENTS

- 1 c. almonds, soaked in warm water for 10 minutes
- 1 tsp. vanilla extract, unsweetened
- 3 c. filtered water

DIRECTIONS

1. Drain the soaked almonds, place them into the blender, pour in water, and blend for 2 minutes until almonds are chopped.
2. Strain the milk by passing it through cheesecloth into a bowl, discard almond meal, and then stir vanilla into the milk.
3. Cover the milk, refrigerate until chilled, and when ready to serve, stir it well, pour the milk evenly into the glasses and then serve.

Nutritions: *Calories: 30 Fat: 2.5g Carbs: 1g Protein: 1g Sodium: 170mg Potassium: 140mgmg Phosphorus: 30mg*

215. CUCUMBER AND LEMON-FLAVORED WATER

PREPARATION: 5 MIN

COOKING: 3 H

SERVES: 10

INGREDIENTS

- 1 lemon, deseeded, sliced
- ¼ c. fresh mint leaves, chopped
- 1 medium cucumber, sliced
- ¼ c. fresh basil leaves, chopped
- 10 c. water

DIRECTIONS

1. Place the papaya and mint in a large pitcher. Pour in the water.
2. Stir and place the pitcher in the refrigerator to infuse, overnight if possible.
3. Serve cold.

Nutritions: *Calories: 10 Fat: 0g Carbs: 2.25g Protein: 0.12g Sodium: 2.5mg Potassium: 8.9mg Phosphorus: 10mg*

216. BLUEBERRY SMOOTHIE

PREPARATION: 5 MIN **COOKING: 2 MIN** **SERVES: 4**

INGREDIENTS

- 1 c. frozen blueberries
- 6 tbsp. protein powder
- 8 packets Splenda
- 14 oz. apple juice, unsweetened
- 8 cubes of ice

DIRECTIONS

1. Take a blender and place all the ingredients (in order) in it. process for 1 minute until smooth.
2. Distribute the smoothie between four glasses and then serve.

Nutritions: *Calories: 162 Fat: 0.5g Carbs: 30g Protein: 8g Sodium: 123.4mg Potassium: 223mg Phosphorus: 109mg*

217. BLACKBERRY SAGE COCKTAIL

PREPARATION: 5 MIN

COOKING: 10 MIN

SERVES: 6

INGREDIENTS

- Sage Simple Syrup
- 1 cup water
- 1 cup0granulated sugar
- 8 fresh sage leaves, plus more for garnish
- 1-pint fresh blackberries, muddled and strained (juices reserved)
- Juice of 1/2 a lemon
- 8 oz St. Germain Liqueur
- 16 oz vodka
- seltzer water

DIRECTIONS

1. Place water and sugar in a small saucepan.
2. Simmer until sugar dissolves for 7 to 10 minutes.
3. Remove from heat. Add sage leaves, and cover, allowing the mixture for about 2 hours.
4. Combine fresh blackberry juice, lemon juice, sage simple syrup, cocktail pitcher.
5. Mix and refrigerate covered until well chilled.
6. Serve in cocktail glasses filled with ice and garnish with fresh sage leaves and top with a splash of seltzer water.

Nutritions: *Calories: 68 Fat: 1g Carbs: 15g Protein: 3g Sodium: 3mg Potassium: 133mg Phosphorus: 38mg*

218. APPLE- CINNAMON DRINK

PREPARATION: 10 MIN   **COOKING: 20 MIN**   **SERVES: 4**

INGREDIENTS

- 13 fresh apples
- 750ml-1L cold water
- 3-4 tablespoons cinnamon
- 1-2 tablespoons sugar (brown or caster)

DIRECTIONS

1. Peel, chop and cook 13 fresh apples.
2. Once they were half-cooked, add water leaving for 2 minutes
3. Add a lot of cinnamon (3-4 tablespoons, but you can add as much as you please, really) and 1-2 tablespoons sugar.
4. Keep cooking for another 5 minutes.
5. Drain and put into the new container back in the pan and bring it to the boil.
6. Add more cinnamon and a bit of water to thin it out a bit.
7. Pour into a cup and enjoy.

Nutritions: *Calories: 130 Fat: 0g Carbs: 32g Protein: 0g Sodium: 20mg Potassium: 0mg Phosphorus: 0mg*

219. DETOXIFYING BEET JUICE

PREPARATION: 10 MIN

COOKING: 10 MIN

SERVES: 4

INGREDIENTS

- 1-pound beets, washed with ends cut off
- 2 pounds carrots, washed with ends cut off
- 1 bunch celery, washed and broken into ribs
- 2 lemons, peel cut off and quartered
- 1 lime, peel cut off and quartered
- 1 bunch flat-leaf parsley, washed
- 1 Fuji or Honeycrisp red apple, chopped (optional, for extra sweetness)

DIRECTIONS

1. Wash produce and chop so pieces will fit into the feeder tube of your juicer.
2. Feed the vegetable pieces through the juicer, alternating harder and softer textured pieces to aid in the juicing process.
3. Serve immediately or store in the refrigerator in a highly sealed container.
4. The juice is best when served within 48 hours of making.

Nutritions: *Calories: 58 Fat: 0g Carbs: 13g Protein: 2g Sodium: 106mg Potassium: 442mg Phosphorus: 54mg*

220. HONEY CINNAMON LATTE

PREPARATION: 5 MIN

COOKING: 5 MIN

SERVES: 2

INGREDIENTS

- 1-½ cups of organic, unsweetened almond milk
- 1 scoop of organic vanilla protein powder
- 1 teaspoon of organic cinnamon
- ½ teaspoon of pure, local honey
- 1-2 shots of espresso

DIRECTIONS

1. Heat almond milk in the microwave until hot to the touch.
2. Add honey and stir until completely melted.
3. Using a whisk, add cinnamon, and protein powder and thoroughly combine.
4. Pour into a manual milk and froth concoction until foamy and creamy.
5. Pour espresso shots into a mug and add in milk mixture.

Nutritions: *Calories: 115 Fat: 3g Carbs: 26g Protein: 3g Sodium: 125mg Potassium: 10.9mg Phosphorus: 0.1mg*

221. CINNAMON SMOOTHIE

PREPARATION: 5 MIN

COOKING: 5 MIN

SERVES: 2

INGREDIENTS

- 1 large banana
- 150g plain or Greek yogurt
- 300ml milk
- 2 tbsp smooth peanut butter
- 1/4 tsp Schwartz Ground Cinnamon

DIRECTIONS

1. Add all the ingredients to a blender and blitz until smooth.
2. Serve immediately.

Nutritions: *Calories: 88 Fat: 4.3g Carbs: 3g Protein: 8g Sodium: 187mg Potassium: 241mg Phosphorus: 20mg*

222. CITRUS SMOOTHIE

PREPARATION: 5 MIN   **COOKING: 2 MIN**   **SERVES: 2**

INGREDIENTS

- 1 large orange, peeled, halved
- ¼ lemon, peeled, seeded
- ½ cup (85 g) pineapple, peeled, cubed
- ¼ cup (60 g) frozen mango
- 1 cup (130 g) ice cubes

DIRECTIONS

1. Prepare all ingredients into the container and secure lid.
2. Turn machine on and slowly increase speed to high.
3. Blend for 1 minute or until the desired consistency is reached.

Nutritions: *Calories: 280 Fat: 0g Carbs: 67g Protein: 4g Sodium: 30mg Potassium: 570mg Phosphorus: 0mg*

223. PINEAPPLE PROTEIN SMOOTHIE

PREPARATION: 5 MIN   **COOKING: 0 MIN**   **SERVES: 1**

INGREDIENTS

- 1/2 cup cottage cheese
- 1/2 frozen banana
- 1/2 cup frozen pineapple chunks
- 1/2 tsp brown sugar (optional)
- 1/4 tsp vanilla extract
- 1 Tbsp ground flaxseed (optional)
- 1 cup milk of choice (unsweetened almond milk)

DIRECTIONS

1. Place all of the ingredients into a blender, and then blend until smooth.
2. Serve immediately.

Nutritions: *Calories: 220 Carbohydrates: 29g Protein: 24g Fat: 0.5g Sodium: 195mg Potassium: 325mg Phosphorus: 0mg*

224. HAZELNUT CINNAMON COFFEE

PREPARATION: 5 MIN **COOKING: 2 MIN** **SERVES: 1**

INGREDIENTS

- 1 1/2 cups fresh brewed Toasted Hazelnut Blend
- 1 cup half & half
- 1/4 cup chocolate syrup
- 2 tablespoons hazelnut syrup
- 1/8 teaspoon ground cinnamon

DIRECTIONS

1. Add hot coffee to a 1-quart saucepan.
2. Steadily add all remaining ingredients, then stir.
3. Cook at medium temperature.
4. Put a sprinkle of cinnamon on top and enjoy.

Nutritions: *Calories: 161 Fat: 7g Carbs: 23g Protein: 2g Sodium: 34.6mg Potassium: 219mg Phosphorus: 100mg*

225. PINA COLADA PROTEIN SMOOTHIE

PREPARATION: 5 MIN

COOKING: 2 MIN

SERVES: 1

INGREDIENTS

- 1/2 cup unsweetened vanilla almond milk
- 1/2 cup unsweetened coconut milk
- 3/4 cup frozen pineapple chunks
- 1 scoop vanilla protein powder
- 1 tsp raw honey
- 1 tsp vanilla

DIRECTIONS

1. Place almond milk, coconut milk, pineapple, vanilla protein powder, honey, and vanilla in a blender.
2. Blend until smooth. Serve immediately.

Nutritions: *Calories: 241 Fat: 7g Carbs: 20g Protein: 26g Sodium: 420mg Potassium: 205mg Phosphorus: 10mg*

CHAPTER 14. DESSERTS

226. PROTEIN BALLS

PREPARATION: 5 MIN

COOKING: 5 MIN

SERVES: 2

INGREDIENTS

- 3/4 cup peanut butter
- 1 tsp cinnamon
- 3 tbsp erythritol
- 1 1/2 cup almond flour

DIRECTIONS

1. Add all ingredients into the mixing bowl and blend until well combined.
2. Place bowl into the fridge for 30 minutes.
3. Remove bowl from the fridge. Make small balls from mixture and place on a baking dish.
4. Serve and enjoy.

Nutritions: *Calories 179 Fat 14.8 g Carbohydrates 10.1 g Sugar 5.3 g Protein 7 g Cholesterol 0 mg Phosphorus: 70mg Potassium: 87mg Sodium:95mg*

227. MACADAMIA CANDY

PREPARATION: 5 MIN

COOKING: 5 MIN

SERVES: 4

INGREDIENTS

- 1 cup macadamia nuts
- 10 drops liquid stevia
- 1/2 tsp vanilla
- 2 tbsp swerve
- 1/2 cup coconut oil

DIRECTIONS

1. Add all ingredients into the blender and blend until smooth.
2. Pour mixture into the mini silicone candy molds and place in the refrigerator until set.
3. Serve and enjoy.

Nutritions: *Calories 137 Fat 15 g Carbohydrates 1.6 g Sugar 0.5 g Protein 0.8 g Cholesterol 0 mg Phosphorus: 80mg Potassium: 97mg Sodium: 75mg*

228. COCONUT COOKIES

PREPARATION: 10 MIN

COOKING: 10 MIN

SERVES: 4

INGREDIENTS

- 4 cups unsweetened shredded coconut
- 1/4 cup swerve
- 1/2 tsp vanilla
- 1/2 cup unsweetened almond milk

DIRECTIONS

1. Add all ingredients to the food processor and process until a sticky mixture is formed.
2. Make a small ball from mixture and place on a baking tray.
3. Press each ball lightly using the back of the spoon and place it in the refrigerator until firm.
4. Serve and enjoy.

Nutritions: *Calories 73 Fat 6.4 g Carbohydrates 2.5 g Sugar 0.8 g Protein 0.8 g Cholesterol 0 mg Phosphorus: 84mg Potassium: 92mg Sodium: 55mg*

229. BLACKBERRY ICE CREAM

PREPARATION: 10 MIN   **COOKING: 10 MIN**   **SERVES: 8**

INGREDIENTS

- 1 egg yolks
- 1 1/2 cup heavy whipping cream
- 1 cup blackberries
- 1/2 cup Swerve

DIRECTIONS

1. Add all ingredients into the blender and blend until smooth.
2. Pour blended mixture into the ice cream maker and churn according to the machine instructions.
3. Serve and enjoy.

Nutritions: *Calories 92 Fat 9 g Carbohydrates 2.6 g Sugar 0.9 g Protein 1.1 g Cholesterol 57 mg Phosphorus: 70mg Potassium: 57mg Sodium: 75mg*

230. STRAWBERRY LEMON YOGURT

PREPARATION: 5 MIN

COOKING: 5 MIN

SERVES: 8

INGREDIENTS

- 4 cups frozen strawberries
- 8 drops liquid stevia
- 1/2 tbsp fresh lemon juice
- 1/2 cup yogurt

DIRECTIONS

1. Add all ingredients into the blender and blend until smooth.
2. Serve immediately and enjoy it.

Nutritions: *Calories 36 Fat 0.2 g Carbohydrates 7.6 g Sugar 5.6 g Protein 0.9 g Cholesterol 1 mg Phosphorus: 70mg Potassium: 27mg Sodium: 55mg*

231. CHOCOLATE CHIPS FUDGE

PREPARATION: 5 MIN

COOKING: 1 H 30 MIN

SERVES: 2

INGREDIENTS

- 1 cup coconut milk, full-fat
- 1 tbsp vanilla extract
- 2½ cups chocolate chips, sugar-free
- 1-2 tbsps liquid stevia or to taste
- ⅛ tbsp salt

DIRECTIONS

1. Line a baking dish, 8 x 8 inches, with parchment paper. Set aside.
2. Pour coconut milk into your slow cooker then add vanilla, chocolate chips, stevia, and salt. Stir to combine.
3. Cover using paper towel then place the lid on a jar, slightly, allowing steam to escape.
4. Cook for about 1½ hours on Low. Turn off then stir until smooth.
5. Transfer and spread the mixture on the baking dish and refrigerate for about 1 hour until firm.
6. Cut the fudge into 25 pieces, equal squares, then store in the fridge for up to 2 weeks in a container, airtight.
7. Serve and enjoy.

Nutritions: *Calories:85 Total fat: 9, Saturated fat: 3g Total carbs: 1g Net carbs: 1g Protein: 0g Sugar: 1g Fiber: 0g Sodium: 123mg Potassium: 230mg*

232. CHOCOLATE MOLTEN LAVA CAKE

PREPARATION: 10 MIN

COOKING: 3 H

SERVES: 12

INGREDIENTS

- Cooking spray
- 1 ½ cup swerve
- ½ cup flour, gluten-free
- 5 tbsp cocoa powder, unsweetened and divided
- 1 tbsp baking powder
- ½ tbsp salt
- ½ cup butter, melted
- 3 eggs
- 3 egg yolks
- 1 tbsp vanilla extract
- ½ tbsp vanilla liquid stevia
- 4 oz chocolate chips, sugar-free
- 2 cups hot water

DIRECTIONS

1. Grease your slow cooker with oil.
2. Whisk together 1 ¼ cup swerve, flour, 3 tbsp cocoa powder, baking powder and salt in a mixing bowl.
3. In another bowl mix butter, eggs, egg yolks, vanilla extract, and vanilla liquid stevia.
4. Add the wet ingredients into the dry ingredients and mix until well combined.
5. Pour mixture into the slow cooker and top with chocolate chips.
6. Whisk together the remaining cocoa powder, swerve and hot water.
7. Pour the mixture over the chocolate chips.
8. Cover the slow cooker and cook for 3 hours on low. Let rest to cool before serving.

Nutritions: *Calories 174.6 Total Fat 13g Saturated Fat 6.4g Total Carbs 10.5g Net Carbs 7.9g Protein 3.9g Sugar: 0.2g Fiber: 2.6g Sodium: 166mg*

233. COCONUT ALMOND CAKE

PREPARATION: 10 MIN

COOKING: 4 H

SERVES: 8

INGREDIENTS

- 1 cup almond flour
- ½ cup coconut, unsweetened and shredded
- ⅓ cup stevia
- 1 tbsp baking powder
- 1 tbsp apple pie spice
- 2 eggs, lightly whisked
- ¼ cup butter, melted
- ½ cup heavy whipping cream
- 2 cups of water

DIRECTIONS

1. Mix all dry ingredients in a mixing bowl until well combined.
2. Add the wet ingredients one at a time ensuring you mix thoroughly with each addition.
3. Pour the mixture in a cake pan that can fit your slow cooker and cover with paper foil.
4. Place two cups of water in your slow cooker and place the trivet in place.
5. Lower the cake pan on the trivet then cover the slow cooker. Cook on high for 4 hours.
6. When the time has elapsed, take out the cake pan and place it on a cooling rack. Let cool for 20 minutes.
7. Transfer the cake to a plate then sprinkle with almonds and coconuts.
8. Serve and enjoy.

Nutritions: *Calories 247 Total Fat 23g Saturated Fat 11g Total Carbs 5g Net Carbs 3g Protein 5g Sugar: 3g Fiber: 2g Sodium: 74mg Potassium: 108mg*

234. DARK CHOCOLATE CAKE

PREPARATION: 10 MIN

COOKING: 3 H

SERVES: 10

INGREDIENTS

- Cooking spray
- 1 cup + 2 tbsp almond flour
- ½ cup swerve granular
- 3 tbsp protein powder, unflavored
- ½ cup cocoa powder, sugar-free
- 1 ½ tbsp baking powder
- ¼ tbsp salt
- 3 eggs
- 6 tbsp butter, melted
- ⅔ cup almond milk, unsweetened
- ¾ tbsp vanilla extract
- ⅓ cup chocolate chips, sugar-free

DIRECTIONS

1. Grease your 6 -quart slow cooker inserts well with oil.
2. Whisk together flour, swerve, protein powder, cocoa powder, baking powder and salt in a mixing bowl.
3. Stir in eggs, butter, milk, vanilla extract, and chocolate chips until well combined.
4. Pour the mixture in the greased slow cooker insert and cook on low for 2 ½ hours.
5. When the time has elapsed turn off the slow cooker and let the cake rest for 30 minutes before slicing.
6. Serve and enjoy.

Nutritions: *Calories 216.2 Total Fat 17g Saturated Fat 8g Total Carbs 8.4g Net Carbs 4.4g Protein 7.37g Sugar: 3g Fiber: 4.1g Sodium: 347mg Potassium 141g*

235. SWEET BLUEBERRY LEMON CAKE

PREPARATION: 10 MIN   **COOKING: 2 H 30 MIN**   **SERVES: 10**

INGREDIENTS

For the sauce:
- ¼ cup lemon juice
- 1 ½ cup blueberries
- 1 tbsp monk fruit powder
- ¼ cup ghee
- 2 tbsp water
- 1 tbsp almond flour

For the cake:
- 1 ½ tbsp lemon zest
- ½ cup ghee, melted
- ½ cup coconut cream
- ¼ lemon juice
- 4 eggs
- ¼ cup coconut flour
- 2 cups almond flour
- 2 tbsp baking powder
- 3 tbsp monk fruit powder, divided

DIRECTIONS

For the Blueberry Lemon Sauce:
1. Combine the lemon juice, blueberries, monk fruit, and ghee in a small saucepan over medium-high heat until well combined. Bring to boil.
2. Whisk together water and almond flour in a bowl until the flour is dissolved. Pour the mixture over the blueberries mixture and stir to mix.
3. Simmer for about 2 to 4 minutes ensuring you stir occasionally until the sauce thickens.

For the cake:
4. Whisk together lemon zest, ghee, cream, lemon juice, and eggs in a mixing bowl.
5. Sift in coconut flour, almond flour, baking powder, and fruit powder. Stir until well combined.
6. Pour the cake mixture in the slow cooker insert and smooth it out.
7. Add the blueberry sauce over the cake and gently swirl it using a butter knife tip.
8. Cook on high for 2 ½ hours then serve warm. Enjoy.

Nutritions: *Calories 169 Total Fat 25g Saturated Fat 8g Total Carbs 31g Net Carbs 6g Protein 10g Sugar: 12g Fiber: 13g Sodium: 50mg Potassium 71mg*

236. LEMON COCONUT CREAM DESSERT

PREPARATION: 10 MIN

COOKING: 3 H

SERVES: 4

INGREDIENTS

- 5 eggs
- ¼ cup lemon juice, freshly squeezed
- 1 tbsp lemon zest
- 1 tbsp vanilla extract
- ½ tbsp liquid stevia
- 2 cups coconut cream
- Whipped cream, slightly sweetened

DIRECTIONS

1. Whisk together egg yolks, lemon juice and zest, vanilla extract and liquid stevia in a mixing bowl.
2. Whisk in coconut cream until well mixed then divide the mixture among 4 ramekins.
3. Place a rack in the slow cooker and place the ramekins on the rack.
4. Add water to the slow cooker until it reaches halfway up the sides of the ramekins.
5. Cover the slow cooker and cook on low for 3 hours.
6. When the time has elapsed remove the ramekins from the slow cooker and let the custard rest to cool.
7. Top with whipped cream, serve and enjoy.

Nutritions: *Calories 310 Total Fat 30g Saturated Fat 9g Total Carbs 3g Net Carbs 3g Protein 7g Sugar: 11g Fiber: 0g Sodium: 499mg Potassium 110g*

237. PUMPKIN PIE PUDDING

PREPARATION: 10 MIN

COOKING: 3 H

SERVES: 6

INGREDIENTS

- 2 eggs
- ½ cup heavy whipping cream
- ¾ cup Erythritol
- 15 oz pumpkin puree, canned
- 1 tbsp pumpkin pie spice
- 1 tbsp vanilla extract
- 1 ½ cup water
- ½ cup heavy whipping cream for finishing

DIRECTIONS

1. Whisk together eggs with all the other ingredients in the order of listing.
2. Grease a 6x3 inch pan and pour the egg mixture into it.
3. Pour 1 ½ cup water in the slow cooker then place a rack. Place the pan with the mixture on the rack and cover the pan with aluminum foil.
4. Cover the slow cooker and cook for three hours on low.
5. When the time has elapsed, remove the lid carefully so as not to allow any water to fall on the pudding.
6. Remove the pudding from the slow cooker and let rest to cool for 8 hours.
7. Serve with heavy whipping cream. Enjoy.

Nutritions: *Calories 188 Total Fat 16g Saturated Fat 9g Total Carbs 8g Net Carbs 6g Protein 3g Sugar: 2g Fiber 2g Sodium: 104mg Potassium 390g*

238. SUGAR-FREE FUDGE

PREPARATION: 5 MIN

COOKING: 2 H

SERVES: 30

INGREDIENTS

- 2 ½ cups chocolate chips, sugar-free
- ⅓ cup coconut milk
- 1 tbsp vanilla extract, pure
- Dash of salt
- 2 tbsp vanilla liquid stevia

DIRECTIONS

1. Stir chocolate chips, coconut milk, vanilla extract, salt, and liquid stevia in a 4-quart slow cooker.
2. Cover the slow cooker and cook for 2 hours on low.
3. When the time has elapsed uncover, turn off the slow cooker and let sit for 30 minutes.
4. Stir until smooth. Line casserole dish with foil and spread the mixture on it.
5. Chill until firm, cut into 30 pieces and serve.

Nutritions: *Calories 57 Total Fat 5g Saturated Fat 3g Total Carbs 2g Net Carbs 2g Protein 1g Sugar: 0g Fiber: 0g Sodium: 10mg*

239. BAKED EGG CUSTARD

 PREPARATION: 15 MIN

 **COOKING: 30 MIN**

 SERVES: 4

INGREDIENTS

- 2 medium eggs, at room temperature
- ¼ cup of semi-skimmed milk
- 3 tablespoons of white sugar
- ½ teaspoon of nutmeg
- 1 teaspoon of vanilla extract

DIRECTIONS

1. Preheat your oven at 375 f/180c
2. Mix all the ingredients in a mixing bowl and beat with a hand mixer for a few seconds until creamy and uniform.
3. Pour the mixture into lightly greased muffin tins.
4. Bake for 25-30 minutes or until the knife, you place inside, comes out clean.

Nutritions: *Calories: 96.56kcal Carbohydrate: 10.5g Protein: 3.5g Sodium: 37.75mg Potassium: 58.19mg Phosphorus: 58.76mg Dietary Fiber: 0.06g Fat: 2.91g*

240. GUMDROP COOKIES

PREPARATION: 15 MIN **COOKING: 12 MIN** **SERVES: 25**

INGREDIENTS

- ½ cup of spreadable unsalted butter
- 1 medium egg
- 1 cup of brown sugar
- 1 ⅔ cups of all-purpose flour, sifted
- ¼ cup of milk
- 1 teaspoon vanilla
- 1 teaspoon of baking powder
- 15 large gumdrops, chopped finely

DIRECTIONS

1. Preheat the oven at 400f/195c.
2. Combine the sugar, butter and egg until creamy.
3. Add the milk and vanilla and stir well.
4. Combine the flour with the baking powder in a different bowl. Incorporate to the sugar, butter mixture, and stir.
5. Add the gumdrops and place the mixture in the fridge for half an hour.
6. Drop the dough with tablespoonful into a lightly greased baking or cookie sheet.
7. Bake for 10-12 minutes or until golden brown in color.

Nutritions: *Calories: 102.17kcal Carbohydrate: 16.5g Protein: 0.86g Sodium: 23.42mg Potassium: 45mg Phosphorus: 32.15mg Dietary Fiber: 0.13g Fat: 4g*

241. POUND CAKE WITH PINEAPPLE

PREPARATION: 10 MIN   **COOKING: 50 MIN**   **SERVES: 24**

INGREDIENTS

- 3 cups of all-purpose flour, sifted
- 3 cups of sugar
- 1 ½ cups of butter
- 6 whole eggs and 3 egg whites
- 1 teaspoon of vanilla extract
- 1 10. Ounce can of pineapple chunks, rinsed and crushed (keep juice aside).

For glaze:
- 1 cup of sugar
- 1 stick of unsalted butter or margarine
- Reserved juice from the pineapple

DIRECTIONS

1. Preheat the oven at 350f/180c.
2. Beat the sugar and the butter with a hand mixer until creamy and smooth.
3. Slowly add the eggs (one or two every time) and stir well after pouring each egg.
4. Add the vanilla extract, follow up with the flour and stir well.
5. Add the drained and chopped pineapple.
6. Pour the mixture into a greased cake tin and bake for 45-50 minutes.
7. In a small saucepan, combine the sugar with the butter and pineapple juice. Stir every few seconds and bring to boil. Cook until you get a creamy to thick glaze consistency.
8. Pour the glaze over the cake while still hot.
9. Let cook for at least 10 seconds and serve.

Nutritions: *calories: 407.4kcal carbohydrate: 79g protein: 4.25g sodium: 118.97mg potassium: 180.32mg phosphorus: 66.37mg dietary fiber: 2.25g fat: 16.48g*

242. APPLE CRUNCH PIE

PREPARATION: 10 MIN

COOKING: 35 MIN

SERVES: 8

INGREDIENTS

- 4 large tart apples, peeled, seeded and sliced
- ½ cup of white all-purpose flour
- ⅓ cup margarine
- 1 cup of sugar
- ¾ cup of rolled oat flakes
- ½ teaspoon of ground nutmeg

DIRECTIONS

1. Preheat the oven to 375f/180c.
2. Place the apples over a lightly greased square pan (around 7 inches).
3. Mix the rest of the ingredients in a medium bowl with and spread the batter over the apples.
4. Bake for 30-35 minutes or until the top crust has gotten golden brown.
5. Serve hot.

Nutritions: *Calories: 261.9kcal Carbohydrate: 47.2g Protein: 1.5g Sodium: 81mg Potassium: 123.74mg Phosphorus: 35.27mg Dietary Fiber: 2.81g Fat: 7.99g*

243. SPICED PEACHES

PREPARATION: 5 MIN

COOKING: 10 MIN

SERVES: 2

INGREDIENTS

- Canned peaches with juices – 1 cup
- Cornstarch – ½ teaspoon
- Ground cloves – 1 teaspoon
- Ground cinnamon – 1 teaspoon
- Ground nutmeg – 1 teaspoon
- Zest of ½ lemon
- Water – ½ cup

DIRECTIONS

1. Drain peaches.
2. Combine cinnamon, cornstarch, nutmeg, ground cloves, and lemon zest in a pan on the stove.
3. Heat on a medium heat and add peaches.
4. Bring to a boil, reduce the heat and simmer for 10 minutes.
5. Serve.

Nutritions: *Calories: 70 Fat: 0g Carb: 14g Phosphorus: 23mg Potassium: 176mg Sodium: 3mg Protein: 1g*

244. PUMPKIN CHEESECAKE BAR

PREPARATION: 10 MIN

COOKING: 50 MIN

SERVES: 4

INGREDIENTS

- Unsalted butter – 2 ½ tablespoons.
- Cream cheese – 4 ounces
- All-purpose white flour – ½ cup
- Golden brown sugar – 3 tablespoons.
- Granulated sugar – ¼ cup
- Pureed pumpkin – ½ cup
- Egg whites - 2
- Ground cinnamon – 1 teaspoon
- Ground nutmeg – 1 teaspoon
- Vanilla extract – 1 teaspoon

DIRECTIONS

1. Preheat the oven to 350f.
2. Mix flour and brown sugar in a bowl.
3. Mix in the butter to form 'breadcrumbs.
4. Place ¾ of this mixture in a dish.
5. Bake in the oven for 15 minutes. Remove and cool.
6. Lightly whisk the egg and fold in the cream cheese, sugar, pumpkin, cinnamon, nutmeg and vanilla until smooth.
7. Pour this mixture over the oven-baked base and sprinkle with the rest of the breadcrumbs from earlier.
8. Bake in the oven for 30 to 35 minutes more.
9. Cool, slice and serve.

Nutritions: *Calories: 248 Fat: 13g Carb: 33g Phosphorus: 67mg Potassium: 96mg Sodium: 146mg Protein: 4g*

245. BLUEBERRY MINI MUFFINS

PREPARATION: 10 MIN

COOKING: 35 MIN

SERVES: 4

INGREDIENTS

- Egg whites – 3
- All-purpose white flour – ¼ cup
- Coconut flour – 1 tablespoon
- Baking soda – 1 teaspoon
- Nutmeg – 1 tablespoon grated
- Vanilla extract – 1 teaspoon
- Stevia – 1 teaspoon
- Fresh blueberries – ¼ cup

DIRECTIONS

1. Preheat the oven to 325f.
2. Mix all the ingredients in a bowl.
3. Divide the batter into 4 and spoon into a lightly oiled muffin tin.
4. Bake in the oven for 15 to 20 minutes or until cooked through.
5. Cool and serve.

Nutritions: *Calories: 62 Fat: 0g Carb: 9g Phosphorus: 103mg Potassium: 65mg Sodium: 62mg Protein: 4g*

246. VANILLA CUSTARD

PREPARATION: 7 MIN

COOKING: 10 MIN

SERVES: 10

INGREDIENTS

- Egg – 1
- Vanilla – 1/8 teaspoon
- Nutmeg – 1/8 teaspoon
- Almond milk – ½ cup
- Stevia - 2 tablespoon

DIRECTIONS

1. Scald the milk then let it cool slightly.
2. Break the egg into a bowl and beat it with the nutmeg.
3. Add the scalded milk, the vanilla, and the sweetener to taste. Mix well.
4. Place the bowl in a baking pan filled with ½ deep of water.
5. Bake for 30 minutes at 325f.
6. Serve.

Nutritions: *Calories: 167.3 Fat: 9g Carb: 11g Phosphorus: 205mg Potassium: 249mg Sodium: 124mg Protein: 10g*

247. CHOCOLATE CHIP COOKIES

PREPARATION: 7 MIN

COOKING: 10 MIN

SERVES: 10

INGREDIENTS

- Semi-sweet chocolate chips – ½ cup
- Baking soda – ½ teaspoon
- Vanilla – ½ teaspoon
- Egg – 1
- Flour – 1 cup
- Margarine – ½ cup
- Stevia – 4 teaspoons

DIRECTIONS

1. Sift the dry ingredients.
2. Cream the margarine, stevia, vanilla and egg with a whisk.
3. Add flour mixture and beat well.
4. Stir in the chocolate chips, then drop teaspoonfuls of the mixture over a greased baking sheet.
5. Bake the cookies for about 10 minutes at 375f.
6. Cool and serve.

Nutritions: *Calories: 106.2 Fat: 7g Carb: 8.9g Phosphorus: 19mg Potassium: 28mg Sodium: 98mg Protein: 1.5g*

248. LEMON MOUSSE

PREPARATION: 20 MIN + CHILL

COOKING: 10 MIN

SERVES: 4

INGREDIENTS

- 1 cup coconut cream
- 8 ounces cream cheese, soft
- ¼ cup fresh lemon juice
- 3 pinches salt
- 1 teaspoon lemon liquid stevia

DIRECTIONS

1. Preheat your oven to 350 °f
2. Grease a ramekin with butter
3. Beat cream, cream cheese, fresh lemon juice, salt and lemon liquid stevia in a mixer
4. Pour batter into ramekin
5. Bake for 10 minutes, then transfer the mousse to a serving glass
6. Let it chill for 2 hours and serve
7. Enjoy!

Nutritions: *Calories: 395 Fat: 31g Carbohydrates: 3g Protein: 5g Phosphorus: 80mg Potassium: 97mg Sodium: 75mg*

249. JALAPENO CRISP

PREPARATION: 10 MIN **COOKING: 1 H 15 MIN** **SERVES: 20**

INGREDIENTS

- 1 cup sesame seeds
- 1 cup sunflower seeds
- 1 cup flaxseeds
- ½ cup hulled hemp seeds
- 3 tablespoons psyllium husk
- 1 teaspoon salt
- 1 teaspoon baking powder
- 2 cups of water

DIRECTIONS

1. Pre-heat your oven to 350 °f
2. Take your blender and add seeds, baking powder, salt, and psyllium husk
3. Blend well until a sand-like texture appears
4. Stir in water and mix until a batter form
5. Allow the batter to rest for 10 minutes until a dough-like thick mixture forms
6. Pour the dough onto a cookie sheet lined with parchment paper
7. Spread it evenly, making sure that it has a thickness of ¼ inch thick all around
8. Bake for 75 minutes in your oven
9. Remove and cut into 20 spices
10. Allow them to cool for 30 minutes and enjoy!

Nutritions: *Calories: 156 Fat: 13g Carbohydrates: 2g Protein: 5g Phosphorus: 70mg Potassium: 57mg Sodium: 45mg*

250. RASPBERRY POPSICLE

PREPARATION: 2 H   **COOKING: 15 MIN**   **SERVES: 4**

INGREDIENTS

- 1 ½ cups raspberries
- 2 cups of water

DIRECTIONS

1. Take a pan and fill it up with water
2. Add raspberries
3. Place it over medium heat and bring to water to a boil
4. Reduce the heat and simmer for 15 minutes
5. Remove heat and pour the mix into popsicle molds
6. Add a popsicle stick and let it chill for 2 hours
7. Serve and enjoy!

Nutritions: *Calories: 58 Fat: 0.4g Carbohydrates: 0g Protein: 1.4g Phosphorus: 40mg Potassium: 97mg Sodium: 45mg*

251. EASY FUDGE

PREPARATION: 15 MIN + CHILL

COOKING: 5 MIN

SERVES: 25

INGREDIENTS

- 1 ¾ cups of coconut butter
- 1 cup pumpkin puree
- 1 teaspoon ground cinnamon
- ¼ teaspoon ground nutmeg
- 1 tablespoon coconut oil

DIRECTIONS

1. Take an 8x8 inch square baking pan and line it with aluminum foil
2. Take a spoon and scoop out the coconut butter into a heated pan and allow the butter to melt
3. Keep stirring well and remove from the heat once fully melted
4. Add spices and pumpkin and keep straining until you have a grain-like texture
5. Add coconut oil and keep stirring to incorporate everything
6. Scoop the mixture into your baking pan and evenly distribute it
7. Place wax paper on top of the mixture and press gently to straighten the top
8. Remove the paper and discard
9. Allow it to chill for 1-2 hours
10. Once chilled, take it out and slice it up into pieces
11. Enjoy!

Nutritions: *Calories: 120 Fat: 10g Carbohydrates: 5g Protein: 1.2g Phosphorus: 88mg Potassium: 90mg Sodium: 75mg*

252. COCONUT LOAF

 PREPARATION: 15 MIN

 **COOKING: 40 MIN**

 SERVES: 4

INGREDIENTS

- 1 ½ tablespoons coconut flour
- ¼ teaspoon baking powder
- 1/8 teaspoon salt
- 1 tablespoon coconut oil, melted
- 1 whole egg

DIRECTIONS

1. Preheat your oven to 350 °f
2. Add coconut flour, baking powder, salt
3. Add coconut oil, eggs and stir well until mixed
4. Leave the batter for several minutes
5. Pour half the batter onto the baking pan
6. Spread it to form a circle, repeat with remaining batter
7. Bake in the oven for 10 minutes
8. Once a golden-brown texture comes, let it cool and serve
9. Enjoy!

Nutritions: *Calories: 297 Fat: 14g Carbohydrates: 15g Protein: 15g Phosphorus: 80mg Potassium: 97mg Sodium: 75mg*

CHAPTER 15. 21-DAY MEAL PLAN

Days	Breakfast	Lunch	Dinner	Snacks
1	Egg White and Broccoli Omelette	Lemon & Herb Chicken Wraps	Vegetarian Gobi Curry	Edamame Guacamole
2	Yogurt Parfait with Strawberries	Ginger & Bean Sprout Steak Stir-Fry	Lemon Butter Salmon	Toasted Pear Chips
3	Eggs in Tortilla	Carrot & Ginger Chicken Noodles	Crab Cake	Citrus Sesame Cookies
4	American Blueberry Pancakes	Roast Beef	Baked Fish in Cream Sauce	Traditional Spritz Cookies
5	Raspberry Peach Breakfast Smoothie	Beef Brochettes	Shrimp & Broccoli	Classic Baking Powder Biscuits
6	Fast Microwave Egg Scramble	Country Fried Steak	Shrimp in Garlic Sauce	Crunchy Chicken Salad Wraps
7	Mango Lassi Smoothie	Beef Pot Roast	Fish Taco	Tasty Chicken Meatballs
8	Breakfast Maple Sausage	Meat Loaf	Baked Trout	Herb Roasted Cauliflower
9	Summer Veggie Omelette	Spiced Lamb Burgers	Spicy Veggie Pancakes	Sautéed Butternut Squash
10	Raspberry Overnight Porridge	Pork Loins with Leeks	Egg and Veggie Fajitas	German Braised Cabbage

11	Berry Chia with Yogurt	Chinese Beef Wraps	Vegetable Biryani	Walnut Pilaf
12	Arugula Eggs with Chili Peppers	Grilled Skirt Steak	Pesto Pasta Salad	Wild Mushroom Couscous
13	Breakfast Skillet	Spicy Lamb Curry	Barley Blueberry Avocado Salad	Basic Meat Loaf
14	Eggs in Tomato Rings	Lamb with Prunes	Pasta with Creamy Broccoli Sauce	Cereal Munch
15	Eggplant Chicken Sandwich	Lamb with Zucchini & Couscous	Asparagus Fried Rice	Coconut Mandarin Salad
16	Eggplant Caprese	Pork with Bell Pepper	Tex-Mex Pepper Stir-Fry	Cream dipped Cucumbers
17	Chorizo Bowl with Corn	Chicken Tortillas	Vegetarian Taco Salad	Barbecue Cups
18	Panzanella Salad	Slow-roast Chicken with Homemade Gravy	Creamy Red Pepper Pasta	Spiced Pretzels
19	Shrimp Bruschetta	Balsamic Chicken Mix	Herbed Mushroom Burgers	Cauliflower with Mustard Sauce
20	Strawberry Muesli	Turkey Pinwheels	Chickpea Curry	Pineapple Cabbage Coleslaw
21	Yogurt Bulgur	Salsa Chicken	Veggie Cabbage Stir-Fry	Seafood Cro-quettes

Measurements And Conversion

Imperial	Metric	Imperial	Metric
1 tbsp	15ml	1 pint	570 ml
2 fl oz	55 ml	1 ¼ pints	725 ml
3 fl oz	75 ml	1 ¾ pints	1 litre
5 fl oz (¼ pint)	150 ml	2 pints	1.2 litres
10 fl oz (½ pint)	275 ml	2½ pints	1.5 litres
		4 pints	2.25 litres

Weight

Imperial	Metric	Imperial	Metric	Imperial	Metric
½ oz	10 g	4 oz	110 g	10 oz	275 g
¾ oz	20 g	4½ oz	125 g	12 oz	350 g
1 oz	25 g	5 oz	150 g	1 lb	450 g
1½ oz	40 g	6 oz	175 g	1 lb 8 oz	700 g
2 oz	50 g	7 oz	200 g	2 lb	900 g
2½ oz	60 g	8 oz	225 g	3 lb	1.35 kg
3 oz	75 g	9 oz	250 g		

Metric cups conversion

Cups	Imperial	Metric
1 cup flour	5oz	150g
1 cup caster or granulated sugar	8oz	225g
1 cup soft brown sugar	6oz	175g
1 cup soft butter/ margarine	8oz	225g
1 cup sultanas/raisins	7oz	200g
1 cup currants	5oz	150g
1 cup ground almonds	4oz	110g
1 cup oats	4oz	110g
1 cup golden syrup/ honey	12oz	350g
1 cup uncooked rice	7oz	200g
1 cup grated cheese	4oz	110g
1 stick butter	4oz	110g
¼ cup liquid (water, milk, oil etc.)	4 tablespoons	60ml
½ cup liquid (water, milk, oil etc.)	¼ pint	125ml
1 cup liquid (water, milk, oil etc.)	½ pint	250ml

Oven temperatures

Gas Mark	Fahrenheit	Celsius	Gas Mark	Fahrenheit	Celsius
1/4	225	110	4	350	180
1/2	250	130	5	375	190
1	275	140	6	400	200
2	300	150	7	425	220
3	325	170	8	450	230
			9	475	240

Weight

Imperial	Metric	Imperial	Metric
½ oz	10 g	6 oz	175 g
¾ oz	20 g	7 oz	200 g
1 oz	25 g	8 oz	225 g
1½ oz	40 g	9 oz	250 g
2 oz	50 g	10 oz	275 g
2½ oz	60 g	12 oz	350 g
3 oz	75 g	1 lb	450 g
4 oz	110 g	1 lb 8 oz	700 g
4½ oz	125 g	2 lb	900 g
5 oz	150 g	3 lb	1.35 kg

CONCLUSION

You likely had little knowledge about your kidneys before. You probably didn't know how you could take steps to improve your kidney health and decrease the risk of developing kidney failure. However, through reading this book, you now understand the power of the human kidney, as well as the prognosis of chronic kidney disease. While over thirty-million Americans are being affected by kidney disease, you can now take steps to be one of the people who is actively working to promote your kidney health.

These stats are alarming, which is why, it is necessary to take proper care of your kidneys, starting with a kidney-friendly diet. These recipes are ideal whether you have been diagnosed with a kidney problem or you want to prevent any kidney issue.

As for your well-being and health, it's a good idea to see your doctor as often as possible to make sure you don't have any preventable problems you don't need to have. The kidneys are your body's channel for toxins (as is the liver), cleaning the blood of unknown substances and toxins that are removed from things like preservatives in food and other toxins. The moment you eat without control and fill your body with toxins, food, drink (liquor or alcohol, for example) or even the air you inhale in general, your body will also convert a number of things that appear to be benign until the body's organs convert them to things like formaldehyde, due to a synthetic response and transformation phase.

One such case is a large part of the dietary sugars used in diet sodas - for example, aspartame is converted to formaldehyde in the body. These toxins must be excreted or they can cause disease, renal (kidney) failure, malignant growth, and various other painful problems

This isn't a condition that occurs without any forethought it is a dynamic issue and in that it very well may be both found early and treated, diet changed, and settling what is causing the issue is conceivable. It's conceivable to have partial renal failure yet, as a rule; it requires some time (or downright poor diet for a short time) to arrive at absolute renal failure. You would prefer not to reach total renal failure since this will require standard dialysis treatments to save your life.

Dialysis treatments explicitly clean the blood of waste and toxins in the blood utilizing a machine in light of the fact that your body can no longer carry out the responsibility. Without treatments, you could die a very painful death. Renal failure can be the consequence of long-haul diabetes, hypertension, unreliable diet, and can stem from other health concerns.

A renal diet is tied in with directing the intake of protein and phosphorus in your eating routine. Restricting your sodium intake is likewise significant. By controlling these two variables you can control the vast majority of the toxins/waste made by your body and thus this enables your kidney to 100% function. In the event that you get this early enough and truly moderate your diets with extraordinary consideration, you could avert complete renal failure. In the event that you get this early, you can take out the issue completely.